The Man Who Launched a Thousand Poems
Volume Two

Selected works

For adults:
Fighting Talk: A COVID-19 Poetry Diary, Vol. 1 †
Can of Worms: A COVID-19 Poetry Diary, Vol. 2 †
Pig's Ear, Dg's Dinner: A COVID-19 Poetry Diary, Vol. 3 †
Nail on the Head: A COVID-19 Poetry Diary, Vol. 4 †
The Man Who Launched a Thousand Poems, Vol. 1 †
The Man Who Launched a Thousand Poems, Vol. 2 †

Touched by The Band of Nod – The Slade Poems •
The Saturday Men •

For children:
Football 4 Every 1 ★
The Very Best of Paul Cookson ★
Paul Cookson's Joke Shop ★
There's a Crocodile in the House ◆

As Editor:
The Works ★
100 Brilliant Poems for Children ★
Fire Burn, Cauldron Bubble ▲

† Published by Flapjack Press
• Published by A Twist in the Tale & available at paulcooksonpoet.co.uk
★ Published by Pan Macmillan ◆ Published by Otter Barry Books
▲ Published by Bloomsbury

PAUL COOKSON

THE MAN WHO LAUNCHED A THOUSAND POEMS

VOLUME TWO

Illustrated by Martin Chatterton

Flapjack Press

flapjackpress.co.uk
Exploring the synergy between performance and the page

Published in 2023 by Flapjack Press
Salford, Gtr Manchester
⊕ flapjackpress.co.uk ▶ Flapjack Press
f Flapjack Press 🐦 FlapjackPress

ISBN 978-1-7396231-9-7

Cover & illustrations by Martin Chatterton
⊕ worldofchatterton.com @ edchatt

Author photo by Sally Cookson

Poems 501–518 were first published in *Nail on the Head.*

Printed by Imprint Digital
Upton Pyne, Exeter, Devon
⊕ digital.imprint.co.uk

FSC

MAN
CHE
STER
A UNESCO City
of Literature

Dedicated to
Martin Chatterton, Korky Paul and Chris Riddell –
you, who see the pictures in the words.

Contents

Introduction

When this poetry diary started, I thought it would probably end when COVID and lockdown ended and life returned to normal. Whatever "normal" is these days.

But it didn't, it hasn't, and here we are. Once we got to poem five hundred, I wondered whether we'd get to poem one thousand. We did.

Journey is an over-used word these days and however clichéd it may sound, that's exactly what it's been. One that I've not made alone.

Integral to this journey have been Martin Chatterton, Korky Paul and Chris Riddell. Martin's designs have given all the books an identity, a visual presence and a distinctive style. All three have brought the poems to life and all three are great friends as well. Even more special to share the pages with them. I do need to mention Martin again though. When these two volumes of five hundred poems each were commissioned, the idea was that he might "decorate" the pages with a few recurring images – like the cover arrow or target. Instead, he immersed himself in the project and produced these stunning results. Commitment above and beyond. Thanks Mart.

What began as a social diary has become my diary. Sometimes social, sometimes political, sometimes sporting, sometimes personal, sometimes elegiac, sometimes just based on a daft pun or joke. But always something.

I love the challenge and commitment. This daily poetical exercise and lexicographical workout. Emotional devotions and everyday psalms.

At the moment, there are no reasons to stop.

To have the thousand poems collected into these two hardback volumes is an immense feeling and a lasting legacy. Special thanks again to Paul Neads at Flapjack Press for his belief and commitment. And to you all, for commenting, sharing and buying the books.

Bless you. You have blessed me.

Paul Cookson
January 2023

The Man Who Launched a Thousand Poems
Volume Two

What Started As A Whisper ...
#501 / 05:07:2021

There's a humming in the streets, a buzzing in the air
Three words of a song seem to echo everywhere
Belief is getting stronger with every goal we score
What started as a whisper has now become a roar

Caution, trepidation, weighed down by the past
And a nation's desperation to make this moment last
All the pain and all the hurt – we've all been there before
But what started as a whisper has now become a roar

Exceeding expectation, unbeaten in our task
A time for celebration – the prize within our grasp
Games completed, undefeated – now it's time to soar
What started as a whisper has now become a roar

This chapter in the story now becoming real
This dream of hope and glory – something new that we all feel
We never dared to dream what the future had in store
What started as a whisper has now become a roar

Nearly there, don't falter now – one match at a time
Nothing much to alter now, things are going fine
Opportunity is knocking, unlocking every door
What started as a whisper has now become a roar

The who and what and why and how, just keep Raheem and Harry on
We don't think it's over now, just want it all to carry on
Let this now be the time when football's home once more
What started as a whisper has now become a roar

A Freedom Poem
#502 / 06:07:2021

today's poem is a freedom poem there are no
restrictions on genre style or rhythm and no
guidelines regarding rhymes on lines internal
or otherwise they are there but it is up to you
to recognise them that is your own personal
choice this poem has words you may choose to
read or completely ignore again that is totally
your own choice and up to your own personal
interpretation should you want to break these
words up into verses with spaces in between
well that is up to you as everything is here and
you can look at all the information and rewrite
the poem accordingly true there is no structure
and the lack of punctuation may confuse the fact
that the words are somewhat crowded together
perhaps appearing a little muddled but isn't that
what you wanted some creative freedom and room
to manoeuvre with no-one telling you how it all
should be so yes this is a normal poem but it is up
to you how to interpret it because that is your own
personal responsibility plus the fact because you
have read a poem on the internet you are suddenly
an expert and know all about poetry so go ahead
be free be free be free be free be free be free be

Sometimes
#503 / 07:07:2021

Sometimes
It's just the act
Of picking up a pen
And putting pen to paper
That makes the magic happen

Three Lines On Those Shirts
#504 / 08:07:2021

One last match, a final step
One more hurdle, one more time
Finally, finally, finally reached that finishing line

Why Wouldn't You?
Just To Be On The Safe Side And Think Of Others
#505 / 08:07:2021

My answer to the question
Should you choose to ask
Even after "Freedom Day"
I'll choose to wear my mask

Fever Pitch
#506 / 09:07:2021

As football fever
Grips the nation
Let us hope and pray
That it is indeed football
And not the fever
That grips the nation

Nothing To Do With Football
#507 / 10:07:2021

We have been living
With the Johnson Variant
For far too long now
All this Brexit talk
And now he just wants England
To win the Euros

Will Of The Nation
#508 / 11:07:2021

I will stand – side by side
Wave the flag, salute the shirt
Celebrate this magic
For all the years of so-called hurt

Enjoy all the euphoria
Give my full support
But I will not boo an anthem
In the name of sport

I will not sneer at those who kneel
Will not whistle, will not jeer
Instead, I'll raise my voice and sing
When my chosen team appear

I will dream of dreams victorious
And all England expects
Whatever happens on the night
Respect – respect – respect

At Last
#509 / 11:07:2021

So here we are
Not many of us have been here before
On the cusp of history
We may have dreamed about this moment
And thought it the impossible
But here we are

Here we all are
United behind a team
Who are united behind their leader
In days when leaders
Have shown themselves to be
Untrustworthy, fickle and shallow

It is good to see a man
Address the nation with respect
Address the nation with honesty
A man not afraid to make his choices
A man with a plan that he will follow through
A man with integrity and dignity

It may be only football
But feels like so much more
The feel-good factor that feels so good
And whatever the score
You have already won our hearts
Already run that extra mile

And should we fall at that final hurdle
You will still be heroes
The ones who restored confidence and belief
And for that
We salute you, Gareth Southgate
We salute you, England

The Morning After The Night Before
#510 / 12:07:2021

Once more the same old feelings
So here we are again
Almost there, but not quite right
Once again – the nearly men

A thumping start to raise the heart
A goal that raised the bar
Despite the hope – we couldn't cope
So close and yet so far

The final hurdle just too high
We've all been here before
We couldn't do the Italian job
And blow the bloody door

Out-thought, outfought, just overwrought
Close but no cigar
The mentality of penalties
So close and yet so far

Foundations, firm and fearless
Lots to be proud about
Reasons to be cheerful
More than usual to shout about

Not there yet – so just re-set
And build from where we are
Learn the lessons from the loss
So close and yet so far

No shame and no disgrace
Not much more we could have done
Perhaps a touch more bravery
And who knows what we could have won

But you have won again the hearts
Let's wish upon this star
And hope it keeps on rising
So close and yet so far

Opposition
#511 / 13:07:2021

The team that we support at home
Have now made the decision
To stand up against all that is wrong
We support their opposition

The team that we all love the most
Have stated their position
To stand together against hate
We support their opposition

Dignity, morality
These men now on a mission
More than just a football team
We support the opposition

Small Change
#512 / 14:07:2021

If you begin with *hate*
And that is all you *have*
Stuck inside that darkened *cave*
You don't even really *care*
So to get right to the very *core*
Of the problem and try to *cope*
Until we bring about *hope*
Could be a journey that's long
But this is the bottom line
We can get from hate to hope
But it might be one letter at a time

Freedom?
#513 / 15:07:2021

As the date draws ever closer
The question is not whether
I will wear my mask
But more
Will I still write a poem every day?

I suspect the answer to both
Will probably be the same

Recipe For Disaster
#514 / 16:07:2021

"The ketchup of the catch up
The yeast that lifts, the magic sauce"
Verbal garnish that's the varnish
To distract from no main course

A mayonnaise to ease malaise
Guacamole to level-up wholly
Salad cream of egalitarian dream
Crunchy coleslaw – less is more

The mustard for the flustered
Horseradish of the mad and faddish
The gravy of gravitas – maybe
The barbecue glaze of better days

The relish of embellishment
A pickle for the fickle
The salt and pepper of the never-never
Chunky chutney for the gluttony

Madly mixed-up metaphors
Keep everybody guessing
Condiments of condescension
All just empty dressing

Common Nonsense
#515 / 17:07:2021

Follow the science
Follow the maths
Look at the facts
The spikes and the graphs
Statistics don't lie
So please may I ask
Is this the right time
To dispense with the masks?

Too Hot For A Hike
#516 / 18:07:2021

Today's poem may be late
I've gone for a walk before it's too hot

A Pilot With No Navigation System
#517 / 18:07:2021

The Prime Minister
Says he is using
The pilot scheme

He is

The Pontius Pilate Scheme
Washing his hands of all responsibility

And has been doing so
For far too long

Freedom Day Sonnet
#518 / 19:07:2021

Cooped up for too long, Freedom Day at last
No longer confined, no more concerns
Cast away caution and chuck all your masks
Good riddance, goodbye, normal life returns

Farewell restrictions, go put them behind
Open your arms to the shops and the bars
Personal freedom for all and you'll find
Chaos will reign in this country of ours

No matter what's wrong, no matter what's right
There is one thing that you must understand
I'll do what I want and go where I like
Rampant and raging, I'll course through this land

On the same page as COVID deniers
Freedom is mine – says Coronavirus

Tanka Very Much
#519 / 20:07:2021

Today
I'm having a
Rest, but rest assured
I will carry on with my daily
Poem

Carry On Captain Chaos
#520 / 21:07:2021

Captain Chaos – creates confusion
Coronavirus crass conclusion
Captain Chaos keeps on cruisin'
Carry on Captain Chaos

Captain Chaos – clearly caters
Crazy crackpot COVID capers
Causing cosmic chasmic craters
Carry on Captain Chaos

Captain Chaos – craving coolness
Conniving, callous, careless, cruellest
Captain Chaos – completely clueless
Carry on Captain Chaos

Captain Chaos – keeps creating
Calamitous communicating
Cataclysmic cogitating
Carry on Captain Chaos

Captain Chaos – crude conquester
Controversial claim contester
King of clowns and court jester
Carry on Captain Chaos

Caped crusader – catatonic
Catastrophic, crooked, chronic
Captain Chaos – cartoon comic
Carry on Captain
Carry on Captain
Carry on causing chaos

The Poem That Time Forgot
#521 / 22:07:2021

Last night – struck down by the muse
Just after News at Ten
So much to write but my excuse
I couldn't find my pen
Worry not, I told myself
I am but a professional
My brain is trained to retain
But here is my confessional
Everything seemed crystal clear
I visualised the lot
But I woke up this morning with
The poem that time forgot

The best ideas I've had in years
Unique and individual
They'll stand the test of time and cast me
As a true original
Cement artistic reputation
Raise me to another level
Gloriously notorious
In new found fame I'd revel
Well I would have – it's no good I've
Given it my best shot
But I woke up this morning with
The poem that time forgot

Turns of phrase that hit the mark
Adopted by the nation
Quoted lines that capture time
A spokesman for a generation
Devastating word play
And the perfect punchline twist
Is that the perfect punchline
Does not now exist
Last night it all seemed obvious
Right now it's gone to pot
Cos I woke up this morning with
The poem that time forgot

Other poets'd wish they wrote it
All the world would try and quote it
National surveys would all vote it
As the favourite poem and note it
Something unforgettable
But what is most regrettable
I'd like to tell you how and why
Who and where and what
But can't recall one line at all
The poem that time forgot

Every writer would have sought it
Advertisers would have bought it
A million quid? That'd sort it
News reporters would report it
Every teacher would have taught it
Every pupil would retort it
The World Wide Web would have caught it
Such a shame I never thought it
Thought I had but not a jot
No bon mot – forgot the lot
Woke this morning with no warning
With the poem that time forgot
The poem that time
The poem that time
Just not got another line
Searching that elusive rhyme
It's a sure-fire certain sign
That this poem was never mine
It's what the world was waiting for
But now it is not …

Cos I woke up this morning with
The poem that time forgot

Value
#522 / 23:07:2021

Value the plumbers and electricians
Brickies and builders, barbers, beauticians
Dentists and doctors, all the physicians
Mechanics and menders and the musicians
Pay them all fairly – they all play their parts
Value them all – value the arts

Value the painters – and decorators
Gardeners, landscapers and undertakers
All of the bar staff and all of the waiters
The butchers and bakers and candlestick-makers
Pay them all fairly – they all play their parts
Value them all – value the arts

Value the teachers and toilet inspectors
Shopworkers, chefs and refuse collectors
Workers on frontlines in all public sectors
Soldiers who serve to try and protect us
Pay them all fairly – they all play their parts
Value them all – value the arts

Caretakers, posties and long-distance drivers
School dinner ladies, lunchtime supervisors
Fast food deliverers, motorbike riders
Factory workers and power providers
Pay them all fairly – they all play their parts
Value them all – value the arts

Join with the joiners, value the planers
Tanners and toners and personal trainers
Thatchers and crofters and stained glass stainers
Dry stone wall builders – plus entertainers
Pay them all fairly – they all play their parts
Value them all – value the arts

Farmers who farm and brewers who brew
Manic street sweepers, technicians too
Cleaners and carers who do what they do
All the comedians who haven't a clue
Pay them all fairly – they all play their parts
Value them all – value the arts

Fishermen, firemen, fire and police
Florists and choristers, pastors and priests
All of the doctors and all of the nurses
Even the poets who write all these verses
Pay them all fairly – they all play their parts
Value them all – value the arts
Cut them and slice them – is where it all starts
Value the artists and value the arts

Don't Believe The Clichés
#523 / 24:07:2021

Some say liars do
Not prosper ... but with you, the
Truth is that they do

"Over the many months your poems have displayed more leadership and sane advice than 60-plus million have received from the government. Thank you." *Richard Cox*

he Time I Take ...
#524 / 25:07:2021

To think of these words
Write them down
Type them up
And edit them
Then sharing on various social media

Well ... I could have done something
Really useful
Like hoovering the upstairs
Or dusting the shutters

The upstairs will always be there
The shutters will not go away
The same cannot be said of poetry

This Haiku Is ...
#525 / 26:07:2021

Not cowering but
Self-isolating in case
The verse goes viral

**A Public Announcement
On Behalf Of The Poet**
#526 / 27:07:2021

Today's poem
Has been cancelled
Due to lack of interest

Not yours
The poet's

Wedding Present
#527 / 28:07:2021

At the time
It didn't feel like a proper wedding present

Gordon and Carol
Mum and dad's next-door neighbours
Gave us a heavy-duty twenty-metre
Rubber-bound outdoor extension cable
With a ribbon on

For nearly thirty-one years
Every time I've mown the lawn, cut the hedge
And managed to get the strimmer to work
I've thought about them
That present and that day

Just goes to show
That although some things come and go
It's the practical that gets you through
Not the flashy, the showy
But the everyday things you take for granted
That's what makes things tick

The cable didn't quite make thirty-one years
Too many re-wirings
And a plug casing no longer secure
It shorted the electrics
And we reluctantly had to throw it away

But we're still here
And you know what?
It is the practical that gets you through
The everyday things you take for granted
That's what makes things tick

Back then
We laughed and were somewhat dismissive
But we were young
Gordon and Carol knew better
That wedding present
This wedding
Present

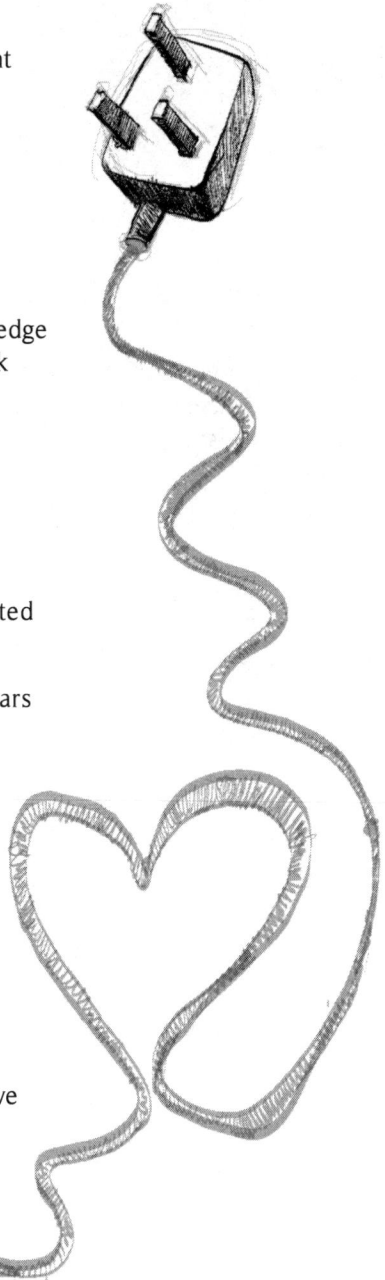

Incomplete Haiku ... ZZ Toppled
#528 / 29:07:2021

One, two ... a, b ...
R.I.P. Dusty Hill
One beat missing

Imagine If It Had Been Someone Else
#529 / 30:07:2021

Man with comedy umbrella routine
Upstages ceremony to commemorate Police dead

Enough said

R.N.L.I.
#530 / 31:07:2021

Really negative loud invective
Refugees not land invaders

Rotten nobody loses influence
Right-wing nothing lacks intelligence

Really Nigel – life's important

Let's Learn Latin
#531 / 01:08:2021

Let's learn Latin! The reading and the writing
Let's learn Latin – ad infinitum
Let's learn Latin … ergo
Let's learn Latin – preserve the status quo

Et tu Brute – persona non grata
Veni vidi vici – ad astra per aspera
Sic, id, est – cognito
Let's learn Latin – preserve the status quo

Let's learn Latin – underfund the arts
Let's learn Latin – this is where it starts
Music, drama, sports all go
Let's learn Latin – preserve the status quo

Work Boots
#532 / 02:08:2021

Dad's been gone
Well over a decade now
But there's still a pair
Of his old work boots in the shed
Steel toe-capped at that

I've been wearing them
For outdoor work recently
Two sizes too big
They get the job done
Still big boots to fill though

Always

It's All About The Lines
#533 / 03:08:2021

Five hours behind a heavy-duty mower
In wet grass
And I can feel it today

Aching all over
Definitely feeling my age
Plus I can't get all the dirt from beneath my nails

Doing something practical, physical
Always makes me feel more masculine
Manly – if not quite macho

I'm starting to harbour thoughts of steel toe-capped boots
And work trousers with loads of pockets
Not that I've anything to put in them

I have an urge to go to B&Q
And buy some sort of power tool
Or, failing that, a big hammer

It's all very well writing poetry
And being the arty type
But is it work? Real work?

Straining to find the best word
Or best rhyme isn't as trying or tiring
As mowing that wet grass down

It's all about getting the lines right
You can certainly see where I've been
It's all about the lines

Just like the poems

Virtual
#534 / 04:08:2021

Virtual and online
Is all very well
Needs must and all that

I've enjoyed the preparation
More than usual to be honest
Thinking of all the gaps and silences to fill

Words needed, carefully rehearsed ad libs
Old stories crowbarred in for ease
Even post-it notes on the right pages

But

I miss the live setting
The buzz of a room
And the energy an audience creates

The rhythm of performance
Reactions and interactions
Smiles, laughter, silence … applause

The spontaneity that responses suggest
The magic of the moment
And the spirit of momentum

One day, this will return
But for now
Virtual will have to do

"Our national treasure." *Judy Camp*

Mad On A Bike
#535 / 05:08:2021

Recently
I've taken to cycling

Today
I wore my specialist shorts

Madonna style
For the very first time

Lycra virgin

Just Checking In ...
And Yes, It's Showbusiness As Usual
#536 / 06:08:2021

Roll up! Roll up! All gather round
Take your seats and enjoy the sound
Of the oohs and the aahs and laughter around
Comedy brollies and japes that abound

The king of the fools is wearing a crown
There's always a circus when he comes to town
Communities shattered and mines closed down
It's all a joke to the Downing Street clown

Haiku Birthday To You
#537 / 07:08:2021

Twenty-eight today
And the body of a man
But you're still my boy

Seventh Heaven
#538 / 08:08:2021
for Sir Jason Kenny

It wasn't just the magnificence
Of your achievements
Our greatest Olympian
Ever

Seven gold medals
Seven
It was your humility
And the respect of your rivals

Holding you high on that podium
Lifting you on their shoulders
Total
And ultimate

Following Instructions
#539 / 09:08:2021

My wife leaves helpful post-it notes
Things to do
Job reminders
That sort of thing

The latest read

Jetwash
Cake

Being helpful and dutiful
I did just that

Now there is a new note

Clean mess off patio
Where is cake?

**Tomorrow's Poem Will No Doubt
Take Stock Of Today In Much More Detail
But For Now This Will Have To Do**
#540 / 10:08:2021

The numbers six and zero
Could make one feel depressed

Overwhelmed and humbled
Lost for words and blessed

What Can I Say?
#541 / 11:08:2021

Today is a day for gratitude
Thank yous and reflection

Friendships are the gifts
That just keep on giving

To love and be loved
Has no price but eternal value

Held aloft by your words
Enfolded by your warmth

Were you all here
I'd buy you all a drink

But as that can't be possible
I've saved myself a fortune

Although a fortune is mine
With all of you around me

I will reflect, I will say thank you
Every day is a day for gratitude

Idle Moments
#542 / 12:08:2021

Idle moments
Give birth to poems
Not all of them good though
Like this one

I'm No Expert But ...
#543 / 13:08:2021

The climate won't change
If the people don't change so
The climate won't change

Not A Poem
#544 / 14:08:2021

I look at the news headlines
And my heart just falls

Writing a poem every day
And I don't want to write about this

But there is no getting away from it
No escaping the horror

So today, I will not write a poem
But a prayer

Only A Matter Of Time
#545 / 15:08:2021

The birthday balloons
Are shrivelled and deflated
I know how they feel

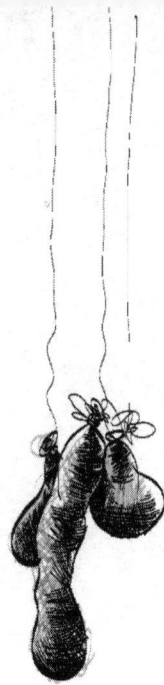

Distracted By The King
#546 / 16:08:2021

I'm supposed to be writing a poem
But my mind is elsewhere
Stephen is distracting me

Committed to a daily offering
But right now, I'd rather
Be among his pages than mine

I may have a brand new notebook
But my attention is drawn
To the detail in the book completed

Nearly finished … that time when
You desperately want to know what happens
But equally don't want the story to end

Yes, I'm supposed to be writing a poem
But Stephen is distracting me
Like he always does

Didn't We Have A Lovely Time ...
#547 / 17:08:2021

The seaside in the rain
Is still the seaside in the rain
August or not

We want lots of water
But sea not drizzle
Swimwear not showerwear

Some try and make the best of it
Sandcastles and kagoules
Paddling with brollies

Dampened families
Overcrowd cafés and coffee shops
Ice cream cones still sell but last longer

Seagulls still scavenge and cry
But are grey shadowy clouds
Against the heavy sky

Some people are in the sea
They think it's still summer
But it's not

An artisan sausage roll
Saves the day, back in the car
Heater on

The seaside in the rain
Is still the seaside in the rain
August or not

Always
#548 / 18:08:2021

This poem has always been here
Just waiting to be written down

Time and opportunity connect
And the words fall into place

Not an act of mystical inspiration
But sheer diligence and physicality

The actual picking up of a pencil
And opening a notebook to a blank page

And starting, just starting
Allowing the words to begin their journey

One will lead to another then another
It is as simple as that

Sometimes almost out of nowhere
They take a twist and a diversion

What do you call a man with a spade on his head?
Dug. Without a spade … Douglas

But mostly they find their place
Their pattern on the page

This poem has always been here
Just waiting to be read

"You are an inspiration." *Sally Thompson*

Afghanistan
#549 / 19:08:2021

...

No words
Except
No words

Unacceptable
#550 / 20:08:2021

There are some words
That should never be together in the same sentence
Like
Bullets over babies' heads at airports
Or
Ministers on beaches in times of international crisis

Constantly Raising The Levels Of Shame
#551 / 21:08:2021

Just when you think things couldn't get worse
They're proving us wrong once again
Upping their game as they move in reverse
Constantly raising the levels of shame

Inept is their best, their worst is disgrace
Always just out of the frame
Nothing of usefulness put into place
Constantly raising the levels of shame

Response and responsible never connect
Never accepting the blame
The only fact this's remaining correct
Constantly raising the levels of shame

Constantly Raising The Levels Of Shame (Part 2)
#552 / 22:08:2021

Missing, inaction – always the case
Predictable, ever the same
Never in touch or in the right place
Constantly raising the levels of shame

Their mouths may be moving but don't speak the truth
Despite whatever they claim
Their lack of humanity, their living proof
Constantly raising the levels of shame

Self-serving, self-centred and so self-obsessed
Wilfully blinkered, they reign
Look after each other – it's what they do best
Constantly raising the levels of shame

Constantly Raising The Levels Of Shame (Part 3)
#553 / 23:08:2021

Too little, too late, too much of not much
Hiding in sight that is plain
When push comes to shove it's hardly a touch
Constantly raising the levels of shame

Morally bankrupt, cold and corrupt
Looking for something to gain
Profit – the cup from which they have supped
Constantly raising the levels of shame

Time after time after time after time
Missing the chances to change
Ignoring the warnings, ignoring the signs
Constantly raising the levels of shame

Sometimes A Haiku Is All That Is Possible
#554 / 24:08:2021

A heavy heart means
It's hard to lift a pen ne-
ver mind the spirit

A Sad Day For Rock And Roll
#555 / 25:08:2021
for Charlie Watts

Sharp suit
Immaculate timing
Not so much the rocker
Always the roller

Backbone man
Metronome heart
Minimal set up
Maximum impact

All that jazz
All that rocks
Knew what's what
Charlie Watts

Punk Rock Gardener
#556 / 26:08:2021

I fought the lawn
Guess who was the winner?
Should I stay or should I mow?
Me? Joe Strimmer

Wheelbarrow
#557 / 27:08:2021

A wheelbarrow may be many things
But it is not a pram for new born babies
A carriage for frightened children
Or a method of transport for aged infirm relatives
As they try to cross the border and escape to safety

And yet it is

If Poems Were Apples
#558 / 28:08:2021

One a day
Would keep the doctor away

In our present situation
That's virtual vaccination

**Unless You Know About Betty's
Then The Penultimate Line Of This Poem
Won't Make Much Sense**
#559 / 29:08:2021

A treat so sweet at Betty's
Cake, afternoon tea
Florentines like you've never seen
Macaroons – to make one swoon
Vanilla slice – oh so nice
And the only fat rascal

Me

Bank Holiday Monday
#560 / 30:08:2021

Since nineteen seventy-seven
Apart from last year, of course

I have spent August Bank Holiday Monday
In a field with Greenbelt family and friends

Not this year though
For one reason or another

One – I didn't book in time
Another – I wasn't invited to perform

Neither of which are problems
It's just the way things are

Part of my heart is there
And wishing I was there

But another part
Feels that it's right to be here

Next year? Who knows?
But whatever happens I know this

August Bank Holiday Monday
And I will always think of Greenbelt

Too Much To Mask?
#561 / 31:08:2021

I'm still wearing mine
If only to swear at the
Selfish ***** who won't

Brand New Year
#562 / 01:09:2021

A year like no other year
A brand new year starts here

A journey that awaits
Things may seem unclear

There may be trepidation
Anxiety and fear

Teacher, pupil, old or young
The time is drawing near

To open all the classroom doors
To all the we hold dear

Embrace these new horizons
Face each new frontier

Cross each bridge together
As challenges appear

Always be a helping hand
And sympathetic ear

A year like no other year
A new school year starts here

Well, That's Cleared That Up Then ...
Or ... All This For A Desperate Pun
#563 / 02:09:2021

I'm sorry that my answers
Appeared somewhat incomplete

Not wanting to be indiscreet
About me being in this Crete

Cabinet
#564 / 03:09:2021

Often wooden
For display purposes only

If the filing variety
Grey is usual

Enough said

Whose Round Is It Anyway?
#565 / 04:09:2021

It was going to be a quick drink
Meet up early
Not stay too late

But things change
One led to two
As things often do

Time flowed fast
Mutual friends met
Strange coincidences and happenstance

And suddenly
Or so it seemed
We had met early and stayed too late

Talked long and laughed hard
No regrets though
Such is the way of things

Until next time …

Today's Poem May Be Later Than Usual Because ...
#566 / 05:09:2021

I'm in Preston
Cooking a roast dinner for my mother
Role reversal

I say "cooking"
The joint is in the oven
And the potatoes are roasting

The rest
Microwave vegetables and gravy
And Yorkshire puddings, oven-ready

But it's still cooking
Me in the kitchen
Not allowing mum to do a thing

Apart from maybe the washing up
Later on
And putting the ever-ready kettle on

We have walked along the sea front
Admired the trees and flowers
Cups of tea and cups of tea

We have travelled down
Memory Lane
But it seems longer and darker these days

Yet the weather is lovely
And it's a grand day to sit out
And admire the garden

Anyway, must go
The potatoes need basting
And that is more important than a poem just now

Abiding Memories
#567 / 06:09:2021

Watching telly with mum
And The Keeper came on

An unexpected film together
The Bert Trautmann story

The prisoner of war
From foe to footballer

The goalie who broke his neck
And played on in the FA Cup

"Don't some people have a lot to put up with
It's a cruel world"

She half-remembered the story
Or the story of the story

And sung along with 'Abide With Me'
The cup final hymn and her church Sundays

This morning, she is still singing it to herself
Abiding memories

Contractual Obligation
#568 / 07:09:2021

When your mind is not on poetry
But you said you'd see it through
Other pressures pressing
This'll have to do

If Idioms Were Truth
#569 / 08:09:2021

Very surprised that
Your trousers are not toasted
After all this time

The Same Old System
#570 / 09:09:2021

The fine details of finance
The question for today
Of course, things must be paid for
Whatever, come what may
Bur who and what and just how much
An area that's grey
Yet the ones who can afford it least
Are the ones who have to pay

Counting costs, profit, loss
Mounting day by day
The cost of living, loving
Things are not okay
Despite the promises they made
And everything they say
The ones who can afford it least
Are the ones who have to pay

They should be offering prayers of hope
Instead they seem to prey
When at last the votes are cast
And it comes to *hey lads hey*
When all is said and all is done
As always is the way
The ones who can afford it least
Are the ones who have to pay

Questionable Answer
#571 / 10:09:2021

When desperation leads you
To make a choice like this
When any life's a better life
Whatever be the risk
Questions may be complex
When it comes to refugees
But the answer surely cannot be
Gunships on the seas

Some Dates Are Forever Etched
#572 / 11:09:2021

On my way back from a school in Barnsley
I stopped at a small garage for petrol
The man behind the counter
Had a small black and white television
I thought he was watching a disaster movie
I didn't know it was the news
At first …

I mean it wasn't six o'clock
Turning the car radio on instead of the CD
Tunes out, I tuned in
Details unfolded as the news exploded
Destruction, disbelief and … despair
Watching the images over and over
On the television at home and it sinks in
This is not an afternoon disaster movie
This. Is. Actually. Happening. Right. Now.
And it felt like the world tipped on its axis
Changed forever

And in a way it did
And in a way it didn't

Fairytale In New York
#573 / 12:09:2021

Once upon a time in New York a dream came true
No fairytale though, not make believe or flight of fancy
Grit, fight, tenacity, skill – a victory against all the odds
History made and a future secured with every move and every shot
Once upon a time in New York – the queen who ruled the court

The Way I Start The Day
#574 / 13:09:2021

A poem is just the way
I start the day these days
A habit I have formed
That I cannot let go or leave behind
The fear that if I do not write one today
I may not write one tomorrow
And the day after that and the day after …

That, I know is not true
I will keep on writing
It's what I do
Even if they were never seen
I will keep on writing
It is what I do
Sometimes it seems that is all I do

Strange and troubled times
And all I can do is sit alone and write
But as one step leads to another
One poem leads onward
They may be read in isolation
But they are all part of the whole

Sometimes it is not what is said
But what is left unsaid
Those of you who read daily
Will know and understand
That a poem is just the way
I start the day these days

In Search Of A Rhyme And Reason
#575 / 14:09:2021

Downing Street's last retort
"Lockdowns are an absolute last resort"

Read what you will with this report
But lockdown starts at the end of aut

umn

A Short Poem Where It Would Seem I'm Not The Only One To Use An Easily Digestible Soundbite Based On A Pun To Sound Like I'm Saying Something Important
#576 / 15:09:2021

He said
Jabs jabs jabs
Jobs jobs jobs

Lies lies lies
Lots lots lots

Pick A Card, Any Card
#577 / 16:09:2021

The cabinet may have been changed
Positions may be rearranged
Despite the kerfuffle
About the reshuffle
Everything stays just the same

The odds have always been stacked
Raab demoted and Gavin is sacked
There may be new faces
But no sign of aces
As jokers are filling the pack

There's A Teacher In The Toilet
#578 / 17:09:2021

There's a teacher in the toilet
We don't know what to do
A teacher in the toilet
Locked inside the loo
She went in at morning break
Now it's half past two
Teacher's in the toilet
Locked inside the loo

There's a teacher in the toilet
Banging on the door
Teacher's in the toilet
Stamping on the floor
Shouting through the wall
We can hear her in the hall
Everyone can hear her call
More and more and more

A teacher in the toilet
Shouting at year six
Blaming all year four and five
For playing naughty tricks
Who has got the key?
Can it be year three?
One and two don't have a clue
So who did this to Miss?
Who did this Miss?
Did you do this to Miss?

Our teacher's in the toilet
She's been there all day long
Pretending that the door is locked
Fooling everyone
She's got a secret key
Chocolate cakes and tea
Till it's half past three
And all the kids have gone

Teacher in the toilet
Her favourite place to go
Locked it from inside
We didn't even know
This is what she does
Pretends to make a fuss
And now the joke's on us
The sneaky so and so

Our teacher's in the toilet
We don't know what to do
Teacher's in the toilet
Locked inside the loo
She went in at morning break
Now it's half past two
Teacher's in the toilet
Locked inside the loo

Because she can't stand you
… and you
… and you
It's true!

Another Post Brexit Conundrum
#579 / 18:09:2021

A vaccination passport
Seems crazy but it's true
But the most important question …
Is it red? Or is it blue?

Often Asked Question
#580 / 19:09:2021

You ask
"What is a poem?"
I say
I don't really know

It isn't a song
It isn't a story
They can be poetic
But they aren't poems

A poem stands by itself
Naked, alone on the page
It lives on the power of its words
Cannot hide behind melody or character

Somebody once said
"It's that stuff
With all the white spaces
Around the edges"

Another …
"If a poem doesn't sound very good
When it's read out loud
Then it's not a very good poem"

It can be many things
Confined by rhyme and structure
Free form and wild
Anything you want really

Intellects pontificate pretentiously
Me?
Just a bunch of words
That you may or may not like

The Word "Legend" Is Often Over-Used
But Not This Time
#581 / 20:09:2021
for Jimmy Greaves

Quite simply
The greatest goal scorer
Of his generation
Or any other generation for that matter

Proficient artistry
The man who was God in the penalty area
You walked on water
Although it was often mud

A record that speaks for itself
And a personality to match
It may be an old game
And sometimes it is funny

But you made it greater
As quick witted off the pitch
As you were with the ball at your feet
Always a joy to watch

Jimmy
A nation grieves

Tuesday Limerick
#582 / 21:09:2021

Well, it's all going spiffingly well
Everything clear as a bell
Some shelves are empty
While others have plenty
As far as my blinkers can tell

Jigsaw Memories
#583 / 22:09:2021

I suppose there's a certain irony
That I'm writing a poem about
National Alzheimer's Day
A day late

It's just that I didn't know
At least I hope I didn't
Age is cruel at the worst of times
And this becomes the worst of times

The jigsaw will never be remade
The pieces are there but all over the place
Some seem to have multiplied
And repeat like an old-fashioned scratched record

Others, upside down, the wrong way round
They don't seem to fit together
Some do connect
But it's rarely correct

The full picture may never be seen
But individual details remain
Occasionally some fall into place
Briefly

More often than not
One is found when least expected
And then becomes the most important piece
Ever … and then isn't

Jigsaw memories
Not in a box
But a sieve
In a darkening room

If I Say It Long Enough
And If I Say It Loud Enough
Then It Really, Really, Really Must Be True
#584 / 23:09:2021

Living standards
Will not be affected
By rising costs
Or money collected

Higher bills
More money to pay
Simple economics
Universal credit cut
Situation chronic

Fuelling The Panic
#585 / 24:09:2021

Chaos and confusion
Who knows what they're doing?
Service station afternoons
Lots of PMQ-ing

Long Live The Muppet Show
#586 / 25:09:2021

It's more than just embarrassing
When a head of sovereign state
Makes a crass and jokey reference
Decades out of date
Never mind the gravitas
For the future world at stake
Never miss a chance
For a jolly wheeze or jape
Dumbing down and dumber still
So keep that level low
It's time to play the music
Long live the muppet show

It's time to light the lights
On Earth before we burn it
It may be easy being green
If you're a frog called Kermit
Not so if you're Bojo
Crossed with Fozzie Bear
Big bug eyes and silly face
Topped with joke shop hair
Jokes that fall and fall so flatly
Did he not or did he
Have intimate relations with
A relative of Miss Piggy?

Again, he hogs the spotlight
Just where he wants to be
Again, he fluffs his lines
No-one takes him seriously
Fooling no-one but himself
Shit creek – we are up it
The show may be long gone for years
But we've still got a muppet
Probably be better off
With his Spitting Image puppet so …
No TV or children's story in this Never-Ending Tory
In the inconceivable, unbelievable, so deceivable, unretrievable
Brand new Muppet Show

Due To Unforeseen Circumstances
#587 / 26:09:2021

Right on cue
And a case of panic rhyming
Today's poem is cut short
(Every cloud, a silver lining)

Crisis? What Crisis?
#588 / 27:09:2021

All demand and no supply
Ever-rising prices
Don't panic Mister Mainwaring
Crisis? What crisis?

Manic Monday Madness
And the government advice is
Everything will be okay
Crisis? What crisis?

That we are all here like this
There are no surprises
The first of April all year round
Fuelling the crisis

Fuelling the crisis
What is more precise is
The only thing we have is
A fool in the crisis

The Shape We Are In
#589 / 28:09:2021

QQQQQQQ
Q BLOCK Q
QQQQQQQ

Don't You Just Hate ...
#590 / 29:09:2021

Jump those who   the queue
And those *push* who   in front too

No Cause
#591 / 30:09:2021

No cause for a panic
No cause for alarm, he
Says while thinking about
Calling in the army

As If There Haven't Been Enough
Problems Regarding Travel Recently
(And also why today's poem is short)
#592 / 01:10:2021

A great day in a school again
Yest still I'm agitated
A puncture in Northampton
Not just the tyre that's deflated

Spel It Owt
#593 / 02:10:2021

The songs we've heard a million times
The songs where we know all the lines ´
The ones that blasted through the charts
The ones embedded in our hearts
We keep alive the name
We keep alive the flame
Friendz, fanz, fun
It's only just begun

Noddy, Jimmy, Dave and Don
Even though the band has gone
Look around at wot they've done
All the memories that live on
We keep alive the name
We keep alive the flame
Friendz, fanz, fun
It's only just begun

All you girlz and all you boyz
We are here to feel the …
Age may make us hazy now
But we are all still …
We keep alive the name
We keep alive the flame
Friendz, fanz, fun
It's only just begun

So look around this room and smile
Thumbs aloft Slayed style
Hear the calling, have no fear
Bak'ome here this time next year
We keep alive the name
We keep alive the flame
Friendz, fanz, fun
It's only just begun

All Us Not So Young Dudes
#594 / 03:10:2021

We may have been reliving our youth
But this time with beers
Rather than school disco Panda Pops
Not just the songs we loved back then
Now we love them even more
Age has given us perspective
We will song those songs
We dared not admit to liking
When everything was tribal
When your band was like your football team
And it was us vee them
Arguments and competition
And when grannies told us
That the old songs were the best
We didn't believe them but now we do
As we relive our youth with beers
Then have a nice sit down for a bit
With a cup of tea

Choose A Poem
#595 / 04:10:2021

Choose a poem
Any poem
Read it
Out loud
Always out loud
Again and again and again
Get used to the words
Feel them roll off your tongue
Breathe their rhythm
Discover their voice
Live the poem
Learn the poem
Love the poem
Go on
Choose a poem
Any poem

I Choose Poetry
#596 / 05:10:2021

I choose poetry
Always

I choose to read it every day
And I choose to write it every day

Some days I choose rhymes
To help me end the lines

And some days I don't
But I always choose poetry

Poetry is democratic, accessible
A pencil and paper and off you go

You can choose to write your own poems
In your own way and style

And no-one can tell that it's wrong
Because it's your poem, your choice

So choose to write poetry
Choose every word carefully

Use them wisely, do not waste them
Perhaps leave some things unsaid

Leave spaces if you want
Your choice

Whatever you do, choose poetry
You will not be disappointed

I choose poetry
Always have, always will

Who Chooses Who?
#597 / 06:10:2021

Do you choose the poems
Or do the poems choose you?

If the latter is true
Some very well thought of poems
Seem to have passed me by
Which is fine

While others have stopped
Reached into my heart
And will not let go
Which is also fine

Call me fickle if you want
But the poems and poets that mean the most
Have warmth and humanity
Accessibility and they speak

Not in heavenly tongues
Or flowery obscurity
They speak my language
Ordinary words in extraordinary ways

If I like the poet
I invariably like the poems
And if I like the poems
I invariable like the poet too

Those with pretention and self-importance
Leave me cold
If they do not choose to communicate
How can I choose them?

Doesn't make me right and them wrong
Or vice versa
Just the way it is
My choice

Poetry Day
#598 / 07:10:2021

It may be designated as
National Poetry Day
But you have the choice
To make every day
A poetry day

Both
#599 / 08:10:2021

When it's all about choice
You must understand
It's not about "or"
It's more about "and"

This Is ...
#600 / 09:10:2021

A poem you will not remember
A poem you will not quote
A poem you will not share
But it is my poem for today

This poem says I am tired
Tired but happy too
A full week of work and shows
Since who knows when

This poem celebrates
The laughter of children
The communion of chorus
And the sharing of the obvious

This is a poem that celebrates poetry
With another poem
And what started as a tired poem
A short idea ... has grown

As the pen makes its own journey
Across the empty page
And leads me into lines
I knew not were there

Such is poetry
Such is the poet
Such is the poem that
This is

So
#601 / 10:10:2021

Never have so few
Done so much to so many
With so little heart

Never have so few
Done so much for so few for
Such private profit

Never have so few
Cared so little for so long
It's now so normal

Never have so few
Words quickly become a so
cialist haiku verse

Yesterday Was ...
But Today Isn't?
#602 / 11:10:2021

Yesterday was
World Mental Health Day
But today isn't
It's probably World Potato Lovers' Day
Or something like that
Actually it's all of these
Native American Day
National Sausage Pizza Day
National Kick Butt Day
National Coming Out Day
International Day of The Girl Child
General Pulaski Memorial Day
And ... Columbus Day
So when you are kicking butt somewhere
While eating sausage pizza
And googling General Pulaski

Just remember that those on Mental Health Day
Will still have the same problems today
And tomorrow
And the day after that ...
World Top Spinning Day

Which may or may not be
A metaphor for World Mental Health Day

800 – Not Eight Hundred
#603 / 12:10:2021

800 libraries – I've written it in numbers
Rather than words for dramatic effect

800 libraries – how many books in a library?
Who knows – thousands and thousands ...

800 libraries – millions of books and resources
Unread, unused, unavailable

800 libraries closed in the last ten years
Access to knowledge knowingly denied

800 communities – countless opportunities
Willingly and wilfully withdrawn

800 libraries gone because of economics
And other priorities

The question must be asked
Can we really trust anyone
Who will allow the closure of
800 libraries?

And Now The News Headlines For The Obvious
#604 / 13:10:2021

Lockdown lives lost, deadly delays
No apologies – Whitehall ways
Broken promises, Brexit blunders
Rising prices, dangerous numbers
Muddled messages – far too slow
Tell us something we don't know

Easel Does It
#605 / 14:10:2021

When things are getting really tough
It's really good to get away
Just get off, just jet off
Far away on holiday
Never mind the mess behind
Leave all of that stress behind
Never mind the shortages
For food and gas and diesel
Just paint a pretty picture
And pose beside your easel

As a leader and an artist
A natural disaster
But as an impressionist
You may be a grand master
Like everything else that you do
We know that it's not really you
But a photo opportunity
Just like one of these'll
Do the job for now
As you pose beside your easel

Another exhibition
But you are no Picasso
Playing to the gallery
We know it's all a crass show
An act designed to distract
No substance and that's a fact
Don't worry about Brexit
The COVID and disease'll
Still be here when you get back
So pose beside your easel

Nero fiddled while Rome burned
You stand with brush in hand
Far away and distant
While chaos rules our land
A masterclass in disrespect
Wilful ignorance, neglect

Isolated, calculated
Wily as a weasel
Condescending mis-direction
Stood beside your easel

The arrogance and sleazy ease
The ignorance in times like these
The ease with which the weasel
Is posing with his easel

Hot Air Buffoon
#606 / 15:10:2021

Gas supplies are running low in UK says surveyor
Yet levels rise excessively somewhere in Marbella

Not A Poem But Respectful Silence
#607 / 16:10:2021

Words are inadequate in times like these
We all share the horror, the shock and the sadness
This is not a poem – but respectful silence

Good To Be Back
#608 / 17:10:2021

There is something about a room full of people
Who have gathered together to share something special
The unity of music and community of song
The sharing of food and just being out – together again

Words and strings, voice and melody
Creators and creation, performers and audience
The magic of those moments, spontaneous and breathing
The touching of hearts in harmonious communion

Early Start
#609 / 18:10:2021

Early morning alarm – twice
Must have needed the extra rest

Early morning poem – two short verses
To be honest, not one of my best

The Ballad Of Johnny Clarke
#610 / 19:10:2021

Zip-style method slickety-slick
Bob Dylan on a stick
Mad Manc motormouth unzipped
Acid tongue Elvis lip
Hits the target hits the mark
Who? John Cooper Clarke

Sharp edge suits back in black
Machine gun rat-a-tat attack
Bird's-nest hair and trademark shades
Twisted turn of verse and phrase
Future's bright shades are dark
Who? John Cooper Clarke

The provocative evocative use and abuse of the syntax semtex
And the expert expositor of the explosive expletive
The how the why the wry the dry the high velocity overdrive
The rhythm and rhyme of a talent sublime
The nicotine baritone resonates pulsates detonates reverberates
The voice of a generation and beyond
Underpublished undervalued underrated often copied imitated
Never equalled never bettered

Human microphone and stand
Rock and roll without the band
A deft exponent of the verbal art
The shatterproof matter of the heart
Finely honed – the art of sarc
Who? John Cooper Clarke

It Has To Rhyme Today
#611 / 20:10:2021
After John Cooper Clarke and Luke Wright.

Arriving at a crowded venue
Much more satisfying when you
Find it pleasin'
The only reason
Is poetry is on the menu

Seven Verses – Six That Are True And One That Isn't ...
Plus You'll Be Glad This Poem Doesn't Have An Illustration
#612 / 21:10:2021

Yesterday was an admin sort of day
Catching up with emails, letter, various jobs
I'd been putting off opening the box
With the NHS logo on it

Being a man of a certain age
I knew what was inside
And therefore was well aware of
The intimate task that lay ahead

A small sealable test tube
And a plastic stick with grooves
Many of you are way ahead of me by now
So I will spare you the grisly detail

And for any images you may currently have
I do apologise profusely ... but
I did follow all the instructions carefully
Especially the line in bold that said

We only need a little poo to test
PLEASE DO NOT ADD EXTRA
PLEASE POST AS SOON AS POSSIBLE

Naturally I did so, anonymously at the post box

Queuing up at the Post Office
With a package containing your own bodily waste
Would just feel wrong
Not that I've ever posted such a package

Unless you count that time I wrote to Downing Street
And that was in a Tupperware lunchbox as well
A special delivery ... plus I added extra
And didn't actually post it until a few weeks later

Chill
#613 / 22:10:2021

A chill in the air
Autumn? Or just the fact that
Numbers rise again

Things are okay though
"Within the parameters"
So says an expert

Limericks Are Usually Fun But This One Isn't
#614 / 23:10:2021

It isn't really surprisin'
That COVID numbers are risin'
All déjà vu
But what can we do
With Christmas on the horizon?

The Blind, They Lead The Bland
#615 / 24:10:2021

The signs are there but no-one takes 'em
Obvious choices – no-one makes 'em
Hibernation – no-one wakes 'em
Rose-tinted blinkers – seem always in demand
Sleepwalking in the dark – the blind they lead the bland

Recent history keeps repeatin'
All self-self-servin', self-defeatin'
Blissful ignorance completin'
Circles keep decreasing like footprints in quicksand
Sleepwalking in the dark – the blind they lead the bland

All these lessons no-one's learnin'
Cos it's okay the world keeps turnin'
Fiddling while home is burnin'
Fires risin', unsurprisin' – all of them are fanned
Sleepwalking in the dark – the blind they lead the bland

With all the effort they can muster
Empty bluff and banal bluster
Fighting fire with a feather duster
In shark infested custard, mixed metaphors to hand
Sleepwalking in the dark – the blind they lead the bland

The blind they lead the bland
They ain't got nothing planned
You gotta understand
It's calculated, underhand

No posts are manned

The Mersey Sound
#616 / 25:10:2021

As an Evertonian
Not the best time to be in the city
Our embarrassing capitulation
Their Mancunian domination

On the other hand
By chance and coincidence
Concerts that I hadn't planned
In easy reach and close at hand

Talking Of Human Waste
#617 / 26:10:2021

We'll find it in the rivers
We'll find it on the beaches

And it always comes to mind
When I listen to your speeches

"Entertaining, topical ... a collection of spirit, humour and humanity."
Greg Freeman

There's Poetry In Them Thar Tunes
#618 / 27:10:2021
for Mike Scott and The Waterboys

I'd forgotten how many of your words I knew
You sang them
And I was there with you
Hymns of my youth
Lines I thought sleeping at best
Suddenly bursting into life

Years slipped timelessly
A favourite well-loved novel flicking backwards
And I remembered how much
I loved those songs
Love those songs
How very much they meant
And how much they still mean

Yes there was rock
And yes there was roll
But reel and swing
Swagger and style
Celebration and style
Spontaneity and showmanship
Poetry and magic
The pure majesty of song

Transportation of the heart
The spirit moved amongst us
Orchestrated wonder
Lightning conductor

All my adult life
Your songs have been there
And tonight
The moon was full
The moon was holy
And together we sang among the firmament
In raptures glorious

Money, Well, Spent
#619 / 28:10:2021

With the money gone on track and trace
You could live in outer space
Banish food banks from this place
Purify all human waste

Exercise a state of grace
Nullify the fear that's faced
For those who live in dire straits
With money gone on track and trace

Open libraries, factory gates
Pay the nurses higher rates
Not give it to all your mates
And other matters of disgrace

The question, now rhetorical
But is it such a silly 'un
But just what good should be done
With thirty-seven billion?

Cheers! Take It On The Chin Chin
#620 / 29:10:2021

No universal credit rise
But savings for the bankers
To celebrate it all
Down with the price of champers

A Poem About Test Results
#621 / 30:10:2021

Bowel screening test results
Got the all clear
Which is more can be said
For the sample sent from here

Another Poem About Test Results
#622 / 30:10:2021

Pinged
After all this time

Apparently I might have been
In the vicinity
Of someone who possibly
Had tested positive

No symptoms
No loss of taste
Unless you count the current band tee-shirt

Smell seems intact
As the visit to the bathroom proved

So I could ignore it
But I've got an event
And even though it's poetry
There may be an audience

So it's important
To do the right thing
With a swab up the nostril
And a seat by yourself

Eventually the display goes pink
Near the capital "C"
And I'm presuming it is "C" for Clear
And not "C" for COVID

I Don't Want A Healthy Halloween
#623 / 31:10:2021

I'm a monster – I'm a vampire
I'm a werewolf – I'm a beast
I dress up and look forward
To this yearly feast
Sickly sweet, I love to eat
My trick or treat sweet dream
I don't want a healthy Halloween

Lots and lots of lollipops
That's what I'm dreaming of
Mountaintops of chocolate drops
Candyfloss – I love
Icky sticky sugared slicky
Fizzy soda stream
I don't want a healthy Halloween

Lantern lit – this is it
Knock knock knock knock knock
Down the street – trick or treat
Then I got a shock
Mrs B at number three
Her trick was really mean
I don't want a healthy Halloween

She thought she'd played a joke
She thought it was a funny 'un
Went inside and came right back
Giving me an onion
Then a carrot, celery stick
And a runner bean
I don't want a healthy Halloween

Cabbages and cauliflowers
Little red courgette
Brussel sprouts, potatoes …
I ain't seen nothing yet
Please no peas! Or things like these
Not an aubergine
I don't want a healthy Halloween

I may be dressed as Frankenstein's
Monster on the prowl
But the gifts she gave me
Really made me howl
Feeling sick thanks to her trick
Not just my face that's green
I don't want – I don't want
I don't want a healthy Halloween

Greta Expectations
#624 / 01:11:2021

Hope is not passive, not blah blah blah
Hope is telling the truth, taking action
Hope always comes from the people
So says a voice of hope

They Say A Picture Paints A Thousand Words But We Don't Need That Many
#625 / 02:11:2021

A man with no mask
And seemingly half asleep
Really says it all

It's A Fair Cop
#626 / 03:11:2021

They make the right noises – use the right words
The clock is still ticking – we must save the world
Don't hold your breath – they're hedging their bets
As they all fly home in their private jets

Normal Rules Do Not Apply
#627 / 04:11:2021

Just when you thought they couldn't stoop
Any lower down
New depths have been plumbed
Further underground
Closer to the sewage pipes
Where the sickening stench is
The steaming stink of sleaze
From the Tory benches

Untouchable, unreachable
But it doesn't really matter son
Descending and defending
A certain Mister Paterson
Who broke the rules for private gain
Expensive consequences
Yet total ease ignoring sleaze
On the Tory benches

Blatant double standards
An outrage to democracy
Deliberate deflection
Wilful, their hypocrisy
The wine of private privilege
A thirst that never quenches
Goes down easy, nice and sleazy
Served on Tory benches

Guilt is not the issue
The facts are insurmountable
Money talks and so he walks
No-one is accountable
Normal rules do not apply
Doesn't matter what we try
Different if it's you or I
They lobby then they cheat and lie
Tory and elite, that's why
They'll be dining free on high
While we are in the trenches

The sickening stink of Tory sleaze
All too normal – days like these
Their corruption guarantees
It's the same old same old story
From the same old same old Tory
Land of no hope, gloat and glory
The con that's in Conservative
That's where the evidence is
Our nostrils clench at the sickening stench
Their putrid sewerage drenches
Greasy, beastly, diseased and weaselly
Sleazy Tory benches

Back-Tracking And U-Turns Fool No-One
#628 / 05:11:2021

Do the right thing
At the right time
For the right reasons

Not a bit later
When you realise
How much you're in trouble

The facts are still the same
The shameless blameless game
And so the fact remains

You did the wrong thing
For the wrong reasons
Deliberately

I Thought I Was Tired Of Fireworks
#629 / 06:11:2021

A lifetime of bonfires and fireworks
I've seen it all before

Once just confined to November 5th
Now, the month leading up to it

Not to mention New Year's Eve
And any old birthday excuse

Fire is just, well ... fire
And fireworks – just fireworks

But here I am, gazing at the sky
Listening to the *oohs* and *aaahs*

The *oohs* and *aaahs* of children's excitement
That punctuate what is happening above

Fire-flowers bloom and fade
Sparkling blossoms dance and disappear

Big bang creations on heavenly canvas
An instant universe with disposable stars

I thought I was tired of fireworks
But apparently I'm not

One Thing Will Inevitably Lead To Another
#630 / 07:11:2021

Lobbying for private gain
Receiving cash for questions
Peerages for donations
Just a natural progression

Looking For A Big Carpet And Brush As Well?
#631 / 08:11:2021

"A storm in a tea cup
Let's put it to bed"
Massive cup
Filthy bed

Joke
#632 / 09:11:2021

So, this bloke walks into a pub
Sorry, not a pub
This bloke walks into a hospital
Sorry, not a bloke
This important man walks into a hospital
Oh, I should have mentioned it
But this important man has actually had COVID-19
Anyway, this important man who has actually had COVID-19
Walks into a hospital and well, walks round it actually
Saying hello to all and sundry, cheekily elbow bumping
And gurning like a nineteen seventies light entertainment
Cheeky chappy, posing for pictures with practising professionals
Who, being fully aware of safety protocols, are all suitably masked-up
And this important man in his arrogance, contempt, wilful stupidity
Complete incompetence and lack of empathy or anything resembling
Common sense or even the act of setting a good example
And can't be bothered to wear a mask says …

Actually, this is isn't a joke
And there is no punchline

I Say, I Say, I Say
#633 / 10:11:2021

This joke
Walks into a hospital

Sick
Extremely

All This Is True
#634 / 11:11:2021

Like James Bond loves a gadget
Guaranteed to self-destruct
Like Mary Berry loves to bake
We are not corrupt

Just like Ronaldo loves to score
Or Dracula likes blood that's sucked
A Pope that loves Catholicism
We are not corrupt

Just like Slade love Christmas-time
Or Mick Jagger likes to strut
A defecating forest bear
We are not corrupt

Rain and snow may fall on down
Volcanoes may erupt
The sun may rise and set
We are not corrupt

Like King Herod loved new born boys
Or Morrissey likes meat that's cooked
All these statements are correct
We are not corrupt

"Your daily poems brighten my day." *Bev Rodham*

Clear And Obvious
#635 / 12:11:2021

All this money – private profit
Still you think – nothing of it
All this money – astronomical
Yet truth is where you're economical

All this money – our deduction
But still you claim ... no corruption

So And So
#636 / 13:11:2021

So
You were asked three times
YES, THREE TIMES
About wearing a face mask in hospital
Yet steadfastly refused

Your wilful arrogance
Your stubborn contempt
Literally in the face of
Safety, common sense and basic politeness

So
If you won't even do
The seemingly little things correctly
Just what does that say about everything else
You will or will not do
And where your priorities lie

Like spending more time
Trying to clear the name of a corrupt minister
Than trying to secure the release
Of an innocent woman

The Black Within The Red
#637 / 14:11:2021

The importance of remembrance
The dignity of silence

Universal symbol of recognition
Poppy, red and raw

I have worn one every year
For over half a century

But for the very first time
Thought about it differently this year

Writing poems with children
We came up with the phrase

The centre, the black dot
Just like a full stop

If only that were true then the silence
Would be longer than two minutes

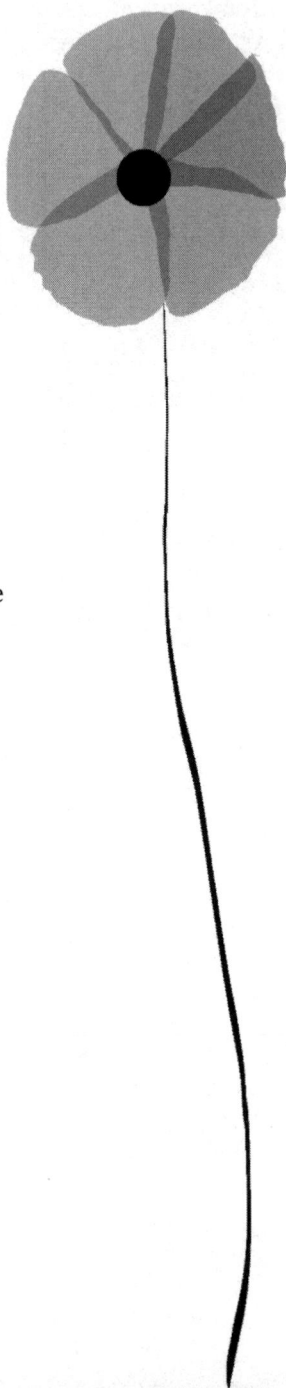

Attention To Detail
#638 / 15:11:2021

Standing attentively
Is not the same as
Standing to attention

We all stood attentively
To listen to the Bible reading
And say "Amen" to the prayers

We all stood attentively
To remember the fallen
And pay our respects

We all stood attentively
To honour the last post
And the laying of the wreaths

And when the National Anthem sounded
The man in the khaki uniform
Two rows in front of me

Stood ramrod still
Tall and proud
As only a serviceman could

And even though I stood attentively
I was not standing to attention
My attention drawn to you

I salute you
Sir
On behalf of them all

Points Of View
#639 / 16:11:2021

While it may be entirely true
And completely accurate
To describe our current Prime Minister
As fourteen stone of tripe
In a badly fitting suit
Who can't even do his collar and tie properly

We must also remember
That not so very long ago
A leading politician was criticised similarly
Due to an anorak and tie combination

So
Are just dumbing down?
Merely levelling up?

Or replacing one set of lazy stereotypes
For another
That just happens to fit our current narrative?

Like A Dog Is Prone To Fleas,
Those In Power Drawn To Sleaze
#640 / 17:11:2021

Solution to the Tory sleaze?
Hand them all redundancies
But they continue this disease
Dot the i's and cross the t's

On deals that grease their wheels with ease
Make more millions as they please
While the country's on its knees
While the NHS is squeezed

They don't care the public sees
Their arrogance in days like these
Sad to say, hell will freeze
Before there is no Tory sleaze

Certainly A Certainty
#641 / 18:11:2021

Face all of the facts
Admit corrupt suggestions
Say sorry for mistakes
And answer all the questions

Yet

You hide behind the shield
Your position has empowered
Certainly no leader
But certainly a coward

A frying pan that's full of grease
Despite it being scoured
Certainly no leader
But certainly a coward

Truth defunct and now debunked
By lies you have devoured
Certainly no leader
But certainly a coward

Accountable for nothing
Honesty is soured
Certainly no leader
But certainly a cowardly cowering corrupt
Conniving crazed controlling
Crass chaotic carry on crowing
Caricature and cartoon clown
Completely crazy coward

Rock And Roll Limericks
#642 / 19:11:2021

A podgy punk rocker in Preston
Who pogoed with just a string vest on
The crowd shouted "No!
There's too much on show
So get dressed and put all the rest on!"

A leather-clad singer in Dublin
Found that the stage lights were troublin'
The heat was fantastic
Conclusion was drastic
The leather was plastic and bubblin'

A tight-trousered rocker in Nottin'ham
Thought he looked sexy and hot in 'em
Like badly packed sprouts
While strutting about
You could see just how many he'd got in 'em

Who Knew Time Flew?
#643 / 20:11:2021

For the first time
Since my birthday
I was officially asked my age

Felt very strange
Actually saying the words "sixty"
In the queue for the flu jab

Although the clue
Might be in the phrase
"Queue for the flu jab"

The Poet Who Ran Out Of ...
#644 / 21:11:2021

The poems he chased day by day
Just like migrating birds
Until one day they went away
The poet who ran out of ...

Rhymes

Logical Conclusion
#645 / 22:11:2021

If I take my wallet
Into a public situation
It is very likely
That I will spend some money

If I take my mobile phone
Into a public place
It is highly probable
That I will make a call at some point

If I drive my car
Out of my garage
And onto the public highway
Then I am definitely using it

So

If I have an AK15
Automatic assault rifle
And choose to take it with me
Into a public place ...

Don't Be Fooled By The Fooling Around Of The Fool
#646 / 23:11:2021

A cartoon man in a cartoon world
Where Peppa Pigs might fly
A jolly good distraction from
The social healthcare lie

All You Need To Know
#647 / 24:11:2021

Those with less can now give more
Those with more can now give less
They could have voted no
But the bastards voted yes

It's Not Much Of A Book Launch If There's No-One In The Room
#648 / 25:11:2021

Apparently
Poetry is no match
For a Christmas market
Late night shopping
A midweek night out
Or Champion's League football

Not even the drunks
Were tempted by a warm room
In a city centre library

Needless to say
Being the professional that I am
I read a selection of well thought out verse
To the rows of empty chairs

No I didn't
I went home early
And watched the Champion's League football

They Are Not Migrants
#649 / 26:11:2021

Call them "migrants"
Make it sound like criminals just fleeing
Call them what they are
Mothers, fathers, children – each one a human being

At Least I'm Only Walking To The Garden Shed
#650 / 27:11:2021

Pouring driving rain that's cold enough to freeze
Icy winds ... could be worse ... could be on the stormy seas

I Am Omicron
#651 / 28:11:2021

Just when you thought that it was safe
Just when you thought it gone
Here I am again ...
I am – Omicron

You thought I was retreating
You thought you had the battle won
Think again as I attack
I am – Omicron

My ever-changing form
Evolving on and on and on
Another metamorphosis
I am – Omicron

Like a mutant in a Star Wars film
A villain in James Bond
So much more and oh so real
I am – Omicron

I'm Sure I've Written This Poem Before
But If History Repeats And We Don't Learn ...
#652 / 29:11:2021

It's important to be vigilant
Important to be on the ball
And rapidly respond
For the safety of us all

Important that we all mask up
And heed this latest warning
And so important that we do it ...
First thing Tuesday morning

Muffled
#653 / 30:11:2021

My words are often muffled and incoherent
When I speak from behind this mask

Much like the words of the Prime Minister
And he doesn't even wear one

"Fantastic." *Mark Cawdery*

Voice
#654 / 01:12:2021

This could be about the usual worries
Masks and ministers
Boris and boosters
But it isn't

It's about my friend
He rang yesterday
Sounding more cheerful and positive
Than he had a right to really

Perhaps he was putting on
A brave voice especially for me
As we caught up, laughed, joked
And talked all things poetry

Conversation drifted into
The realms of blood tests
Inconclusive results
Therefore, more blood tests soon

But at no point
Was there any hint of self-pity
In fact, at one point
He had asked more about me

But that's the way he is
Heart as big as Liverpool
Grace, even bigger
Gabriel's spirit, Solomon's wisdom

I should have been cheering him up
But as usual
He flipped it all
And I felt better for hearing his voice

In so, so many ways

The Usual Let Downs
#655 / 02:12:2021

Don't want to write a poem today
Everton – blown away

Oh – and Boris had a Christmas do
Okay for him, not for you

Billy Is A Pun Rocker
#656 / 03:12:2021
for Billy Bragg

You put the fun in fundamental
The social in the socialist
The cause that's in because
It's not futile to resist
Quip-witted on the uptake
Not just a leftie shocker
Billy was
Billy is
Billy the pun rocker

The small *p* in political
Truth – stronger than fiction
A red Bragg to the bullshit
Delivered with conviction
Ernie the milkman of human kindness
Extra pint doorstopper
Billy was
Billy is
Billy the pun rocker

No-nonsense, common-sense approach
Never diatribal
BBPC evangelist
Reaching for revival
Survival of the wittiest
A bloke both good and proper

Billy was
Billy is
Billy the pun rocker

Empathy for the developing
Don't just read what you believe
Sentimental healthcare
The open art upon your sleeve
A man for all the seasons
On the go and no-show stopper
Billy was
Billy is
Billy the pun rocker
If Billy Bonds could play guitar
Every song a hammer blow
With the cultured Trevor Brooking singing
Drifting on the left wing though
The boy done good, we knew he would
He's got it in his locker
Billy was
Billy is
Billy the pun rocker

The hum that's in humility
You hear what's in the heart
The words we sing along with you
Show strength and that's a start
Enema of the state
Prodder and un-blocker
Solidarity, hilarity
Preaching love and parity
Faith and hope and charity
A cup of tea and clarity
Billy was
Billy is
All the pop
All the fizz
Woody Guthrie Billy Whizz
Just because
Billy is
Billy the pun rocker

"This is really good Paul. Thanks mate." *Billy Bragg*

As We Were And As We Are
#657 / 04:12:2021

With friends in an actual pub
For the first time in over two years

On the one hand it feels ages
On the other like we'd never been away

Our annual get together and catch up
Family, football, fun and friendship

Where once we talked of babies and schools
Now the conversation turns to retirement plans

Weight gain, hair loss, varifocals
And age-appropriate ailments

Once we'd start at eight
And talk and drink till late

Now it's six and back for half-ten
Equally great

And in a way
It is as it always was and always is

Friends catching
Picking up from where we left off

And we will all do the same next year
God willing

"COVID Pill To Be Rolled Out Before Christmas"
#658 / 05:12:021
From a Daily Telegraph headline.

One can only assume
The fact it actually has to be rolled out
Suggests that this is much, much larger
Than a standard pill

If so
How many people does it take
To roll out such a pill?
And surely, if this is the case
There will be distribution problems
Necessitating extra-large lorries and trucks ...

Not to mention
The difficulties actually taking
Such a rolled-out pill

So many unanswered questions
As usual

This Could Go On Anon
#659 / 06:12:2021

An anonymous source revealed anonymously
That people who shall remain anonymous
Attended an event that shall remain anonymous

In an effort to protect their anonymity
The anonymous source would not specify
The nature of the anonymous gathering

Should proceedings proceed this may adversely affect
The anonymity of those individuals anonymously attending
But apparently retrospective offences are not investigated

Especially when they involve the importantly anonymous
According to an ominous source

Probably Best To Get Your Own
House Of Commons In Order First
#660 / 07:12:2021

A ten-year war on drugs, the PM's latest claim
Eleven out of twelve loos – traces of cocaine

Surely Not A Laughing Matter
#661 / 08:12:2021

What did or not happen, we simply have not got the time
For a full investigation on retrospective crime

Just Do What You Want
#662 / 09:12:2021

Just do what you want – it's okay
You even ignore the things that you say
You joke about parties you "never attended"
Don't care about all you may have offended
Who followed the government guidelines suggested
Didn't see loved ones in times that were festive
You do what you want – oh you do
And still the public are voting for you

Do what you want – it's okay
Despite all the negligence that's on display
You like to keep us all in our places
Now you're laughing right in our faces
Utterly callous and total contempt
These are the values that you represent
You do what you want – oh you do
And still the public are voting for you

Just do what you want – it's okay
We'll vote for you next time – oh come what may
You make your own rules up and change them
We don't seem to mind that you rearrange them

Pass all the contracts to all of your mates
Make sure that you get them the very best rates
Yes, do what you want – oh you do
And still the public are voting for you

Just do what you want – it's okay
The stance that you take takes you further away
There's no us and them but just them
Who clearly don't care what happens and when
You claim what you can, whatever amount
Yet nobody's ever been held to account
Yes do what you want – as you do
And still the public are voting for you

Do what you want – it's okay
It seems like you Tories are all here to stay
And the stories, the sleaze and the lies
Are just not enough to dislodge your disguise
The clown and the bumbling buffoon
We've all seen a better dressed circus baboon
Yes, do what you want – like you do
And still the public are voting for you

Do what you want – it's okay
Whatever the crime there's no price to pay
You defecate down from on high
And no-one is shouting out loud enough "Why?"
Never have you lot been so far removed
From everyday values as all this has proved
Yes, do what you want – like you do
And still the public are voting for you

Do what you want – it's okay
You'll do what you have to to get your own way
Just how much more will you make?
Just how much more will we have to take?
Yes, do what you want – like you do
But sooner or later we'll all see what's true

Sooner or later, coming for you
Sooner or later, gunning for you
So do what you want – as you will
But your time is numbered, we're in for the kill

**I Bet The Prime Minister Suddenly Believes
In Social Distances And Self-Isolation**
#663 / 10:12:2021

That way
He wouldn't have to talk to anyone
Or face embarrassing and difficult questions
About all the lies, corruption, sleaze
And daily failings

**Do We Have To Spell It Out
To You, Prime Minister?**
#664 / 11:12:2021

Totally
Without
Any
Trustworthiness

Surely
#665 / 12:12:2021

It being Sunday
I will try to exercise
A certain degree of Christian charity

Surely, all you members
Of the current Conservative party
Can't be as useless as the ones we regularly see

Surely, even you are embarrassed
By the recent shenanigans
Double standards and callous disregard

Surely, some of you must be
Decent human beings with decent values
Who care about other people

Surely, some of you must value
The NHS as the NHS
And not a saleable asset for private gain

Surely, you must be sick
Of the blithering buffoon
And his ever-expanding circus

Surely, surely, surely
At least some of the above may be true
So why not show it to be so

Or are you just waiting
Hoping that it's you or your friends
Who get the next contract or handout

Surely not

Booster
#666 / 13:12:2021

The only booster
He is bothered about is
A boost in ratings

On One Level It Sounds Reasonable
But Then Again ...
#667 / 14:12:2021

All the billions wasted
On contracts for PPE
And now he wants volunteers
To help the NHS out for free

A Statement On Behalf Of The Poetry Minister
#668 / 15:12:2021

In line with current government thinking
This poem
Has been rushed out
With no clear structure

It contains words used before
And clichés to get the job done
But has no idea
A – about the job
Or B – how to do it

It is muddled and confusing
Not knowing whether to be serious
Or contain jokes, puns
And has no rhyme or raisin

The information it gives is non-existent
And it will be forgotten immediately
If not sooner
But it is today's poem

Tomorrow's poem
Will no doubt contradict this poem

Expert Advice
#669 / 16:12:2021

Restrict your social
Interaction says man who
Has never done so

A Nice Surprise
And A Diversion From All Things Political
#670 / 17:12:2021

Expectations lowered
So where did that come from?
A young team, against the odds
Chelsea 1 – Everton 1

Swings And Roundabouts
#671 / 18:12:2021

A swing has momentum
To and fro
Backwards and forwards
Up and down

This was not a swing
No fro
No backwards
Only down

Not really a swing
More a massive shift
In momentum
And public feeling

A roundabout way
Of a total vote of
No confidence
Whatsoever

It Isn't Really Christmas Until Noddy Starts To Sing
#672 / 19:12:2021

Carols sung by candlelight
Festivities at Yule
Children dressed in tea towels
Nativities at school
A manger and a baby
Shepherds and three kings
But it isn't really Christmas
Until Noddy starts to sing

Mistletoe and wine that's mulled
Party celebrations
Lights that never seem to work
Cards and decorations
Chocolate coins hang on the tree
Tinsel glittering
But it isn't really Christmas
Until Noddy starts to sing

Last minute panic buying
Presents round the tree
Children cry in superstores
Sat on Santa's knee
Gran's been on the sherry
Family gatherings
But it isn't really Christmas
Until Noddy starts to sing

Wonky paper hats
Rubbish cracker jokes
The jumper granny knitted
Dinner with the folks
Three balloons suggestively
Hanging on a string
But it isn't really Christmas
Until Noddy starts to sing

Snowmen bringing snow for all
Reindeers with red snouts
The smell of roasted turkey
And the pong of Brussels sprouts

Stockings hanging on the wall
For presents Santa brings
But it isn't really Christmas
Until Noddy starts to sing

Familiar words and melodies
As we all sing along
Rock and roll and festive hymns
All our favourite songs
New York Fairy Tales
And that one of Bing's
But it isn't really Christmas
Until Noddy starts to sing

Eric, Ernie, Mister Preview
The sunshine never stops
Slade and Mud and Wizzard
On Top of the Pops
Gorillas dance on roller skates
Guitars and angel wings
But it isn't really Christmas
Until Noddy starts to sing

Dave Hill the human Christmas tree
The Christmas Number One
Les Gray's Elvis tongue in cheek
Everybody's having fun
This Christmas isn't lonely
With these, my favourite things
And Christmas, yes it's Christmas
When Noddy starts to sing

The ghost of Christmas past
Lives on and on and on
Looking to the future
And it's only just begun
Officially, it's Christmas
So let our anthems ring
So here it is – it's Christmas
When Noddy starts to sing ...

Distracted
#673 / 20:12:2021

The way that things are going
My mind is not on poems

More last-minute preparations
Adjusting lights and decorations

Posting cards, written quickly here
For friends who didn't send one last year

Shopping trips for things we missed
Yet another thing for another list

Trying to find the turkey tin
The Christmas tip on the outside bin

Have we got enough Sellotape?
Can't find the end – for goodness sake!

All of these and much, much more
A hundred things I've missed, for sure

Distracted by this busy season
Not much time for rhyme, the reason

Is that once it's Boxing Day
All of this will have gone away

And I can sit down and relax
And properly write a poem

'Tis The Season ...
#674 / 21:12:2021

'Tis the season to be careful
Thinking of all fellow men
But ...
'Tis the season to be jolly
If you live at Number Ten
Folly – lolly – lie
La – la – la – lie

I'm Sorry To Be Going On About This But ...
#675 / 22:12:2021

While we social distanced
You didn't

While we didn't gather together
You did

While we missed funerals
And care home visits

Special occasions, birthdays
Or just casual get togethers

You didn't
You carried on

Like you just don't care
Like you always do

And then lied about it
Like you always do

Now you ask us to follow guidelines
That you didn't

While delaying action and saying
You won't hesitate to act

It's all going very well
Isn't it?

Déjà Yule
#676 / 23:12:2021

It's beginning to
Feel a lot like Christmas … well
Last Christmas that is

Stay Away From The Manger
#677 / 24:12:2021

Stay away from the manger
Is what teacher said
Last year our Lord Jesus
Was dropped on his head
So Mary hit Joseph
Who then tripped a sheep
The shepherds and wise men
Fell down in a heap

The donkey fell over
And rolled off the stage
On to the piano
As Miss turned the page
The lid on her fingers
Came down with a *CRACK!*
The words that she shouted
Were heard at the back

So this year the infants
Are not in the show
They all said "Pleeeaaassse"
But teacher said "No!
Stay away from the manger
You're not going to spoil it
By waving at parents
And wanting the toilet!"

There Is Always An Empty Place
Around The Christmas Table
#678 / 25:12:2021

There is always an empty place
Around the Christmas table
Someone who should be present
But isn't

Sometimes geography
Sometimes health
Sometimes mortality itself
Sometimes just choice and differences

But there is always an empty place
Around the Christmas table
One cracker not pulled
One hat not worn

It isn't just another day
But at the end of the day, it is
Twenty-four hours from now
All this will pass and we move on

But there is always an empty place
Around the Christmas table
One gift unopened
And an extra portion of turkey

Peace and good will to all men
And joy to the world
Are all very well
But it doesn't always work like that

When there is always am empty place
Around the Christmas table

Boxing Day
#679 / 26:12:2021

Let us gather all our sorrows
All our fears for tomorrows
All our hurting, all our pain
Never to be seen again
Locked into a box and cast away
That would be a perfect Boxing Day

A Saint Of Our Times
#680 / 27:12:2021
for Bishop Desmond Tutu

A saint of our times
And a guide unto our paths
An example to us all
Humility in action

Light and love
Justice and joy
Heart and hope
Mischief and wisdom

The right in righteous
Respected by all
Guided by glory
While walking among us

He knew where he was going
Dancing with the angels now
Earth may be poorer
Heaven can only be richer

On Waking Each Morning When England Are Playing Test Cricket In Australia
#681 / 28:12:2021

Optimism gone
Hope plummets then it crashes
Not much of a test
England and The Ashes

A stern examination
That no-one ever passes
Fail, fail, fail
England and The Ashes

No battle and no fight
No titanic clashes
Sunk without a trace
England and The Ashes

Spineless and pathetic
An embarrassment of hashes
Predictable and weak
England and The Ashes

Blown away like matchsticks
Firewood that crashes
England's reputation
Burning in the Ashes

Been And Gone
#682 / 29:12:2021

Awoken by flashing lights
And banging outside

Not the police, thank goodness
Only the bin men

Only the bin men!
What day is it?

This isn't their usual day
Christmas and New Year schedule

Stuck with a full Christmas bin
Until … who knows when?

Awoken by flashing lights
Bin and gone

Utter Madness
#683 / 30:12:2021

Protesting protesters protest
Intimidate those who seek to protect

Criminal damage to medical sites
Demanding freedom and respect

The Last Poem Of The Year
#684 / 31:12:2021

Could really be any poem from the last year
Nearly two years, to be honest

We are still facing the same issues
And have the same problems to deal with

COVID is still here
Yet still we are led by indecision

Levelling up still favours those
Who are already more level than others

A wealthy man is not sweating
While no-one believes him to be innocent

Anti-vaxxers boo and hiss and scare children
With their pantomime "oh no it isn't"

Thirty-seven billion, yes thirty-seven billion
Thirty-seven actual billion pounds spent

Imagine what that could have been spent on
Imagine what good it could have done

But we are still here, banging the same drum
Writing the same poems over and over again

The last poem of this year could just as well be
The first poem of next year

Resolution Or Re Solution
#685 / 01:01:2022

Let this be a beginning
When we listen to each other
Take on board the wisdom on offer
And not raise our own voices

Let this be a fresh start
With optimism our guardian
Hope our friend
And the words of others our support

Let this be a new slate
A time for silence and reflection
A pause for thought before volume
Safety before sound

Yes, from now on, let us listen
Happy New Year
Sorry, did I say "year"?
I meant let's have a happy new ear

Honourable Sir Or Dishonourable Slur?
#686 / 02:01:2022

Call me old fashioned
Cal me naïve
But New Years and honours
And those who receive

Should be for honour
Achievement or awe
Like the saving of lives
Not starting a war

Already It Seems Like A Long Time Ago
#687 / 03:01:2022

I know it's not the twelfth day
But we've had enough really

The lights are down
Wound up and un-knotted

The tree dismembered
Bagged up and now at the tip

All the decorations are boxed up
And back in the loft

Cards recycled, having ticked off
Who did or didn't send this year

Depositing bottles at the bank
Took longer than usual

We are down to the cheap sweets
And the snacks not good enough for visitors

This is what is left over
These are the remnants of Christmas

These are the signs that Christmas happened
These – and finding pine needles everywhere

Pine Needles
#688 / 04:01:2022

The tree is gone
Having spent all its time looking lovely
In the corner of the living room

But here we are
Finding pine needles
In places it has never been

Kitchen, dining room
Dining room sofa, back bedroom
Even the upstairs bathroom floor

We may hoover
But never seem to get them all
Always at least one more

A stubborn reminder
And the refusal to forget
That Christmas was here

And that maybe
We should keep its spirit
For just a little bit longer

Don't Wanna Be A Cannibal In Space
#689 / 05:01:2022
From a Daily Star headline: "Cannibals in Space".

If space is now the venue
Then you could be on the menu
Flesh that's fresh upon a lunar base
One day perhaps consumin'
A steak that once was human
Don't wanna be a cannibal in space

Like a Soylent Green-based biscuit
Dare you really risk it
And be a human brisket basket case?
I'd be saying "pleased to meat you"
Then thinking how I'd eat you
Don't wanna be a cannibal in space

Human beans on toast
Or astro-nut based roast
No torso morsel ever goes to waste
I wouldn't want first dibs
On sweetbreads or spare ribs
Don't wanna be a cannibal in space

Neither would I linger
On a fishy human finger
A chipolata sausage – just bad taste
Thoughts may turn to murder
Just for a bigger burger
Don't wanna be a cannibal in space

Survival of the fittest
With the serving of the fattest
Don't be the last one in this human race
It's bad enough on Earth
We don't know what things are worth
Don't wanna be a cannibal in space

It's dog eat dog down here
An unhealthy atmosphere
Where everything has lost its rightful place

Already at each other
One thing leads to another
Don't wanna be a cannibal …
A selfish hunting animal
Whether it's down here or up in space

Reasons To Be Cheerless And Depressed
#690 / 06:01:2022

Boris thinks that he knows what is best
Never has a minister known less
Crisis in the NHS
Reasons to be cheerless and depressed
All of those who voted Brexit "yes"
Won't admit it's all a bloody mess
Crisis in the NHS
Reasons to be cheerless and depressed
A sex offender who will not confess
And doesn't seem to sweat like all the rest
Crisis in the NHS
Reasons to be cheerless and depressed
Food banks needed for all those with less
North and south and Midlands, east and west
Crisis in the NHS
Reasons to be cheerless and depressed
No attempt to balance or redress
The gap between the have-nots and the blessed
Crisis in the NHS
Reasons to be cheerless and depressed
Billions are wasted on a test
And still they choose that they will not invest
Crisis in the NHS
Reasons to be cheerless and depressed
Some days I lose all interest
Cannot see the point of getting dressed
Crisis in the NHS
Reasons to be cheerless and depressed

The Last Mince Pie
#691 / 07:01:2022

The turkey has now gone for good
Same can be said for the Christmas pud
Wave the cranberry sauce goodbye
I'm down to the last mince pie

The only biscuits left are plain
Only the coffee crèmes remain
You can see how hard I try
I'm down to the last mince pie

Not a trace of a tangerine
Dates are nowhere to be seen
Likewise the custard, cream and I
Am down to the last mince pie

Gone are the specialist nuts and snacks
The red and green festive packs
And even though a little dry
I'm down to the last mince pie

The smelly cheese is all that's here
The Christmas cake will last all year
No left overs left to fry
I'm down to the last mince pie

There is one unopened box
Of the cheapest market chocs
I think I'll let it pass me by
But I'm down to the last mince pie

Down to the last, the very last
All this feasting, time to fast
Now that this excess has passed
The extra pounds I have amassed
My waistband cannot lie
So …
Hooray for the last mince pie

A Matter Of National Importance
#692 / 08:01:2022

Hospitals can't take the strain
Same mistakes repeat again
But the burning question seems to be
The National Anthem on the BBC

COVID hasn't come and gone
Omicron keeps marching on
But the pressing matter evidently
The National Anthem on the BBC

More important matters in hand
Pain and sorrow throughout the land
But the answer needed immediately
The National Anthem on the BBC

It won't change a single thing
Nobody will stand or sing
Got to be worth the licence fee
The National Anthem on the BBC

The NHS may lie in tatters
But get to the heart of just what matters
What is your priority?
The National Anthem on the BBC

**I Woke Up This Morning
And It Wasn't All A Dream**
#693 / 09:01:2022

Usually on a Sunday
I wake up with the sporting blues
But Everton still won
And England didn't lose

It's Always Alright For Some
#694 / 10:01:2022

Does your flat require updating?
Are your sofa's looking old?
Do your stables need some heating?
Are your horses getting cold?

Worry not, there's funding
From an endless flowing cup
And the taxpayers will help
As we all level up

Join The Conservatives
#695 / 11:01:2022

Look on the lighter brighter side
Do not be downhearted
We put the party in politics
Let's get the party started

Boris Johnson's Wig Stunt Double
#696 / 12:01:2022

You know that things are serious
You know they are in trouble
If in doubt – they call him out
Boris Johnson's wig stunt double

A fabricating Fabricant
Who'll meddle in this muddle
Want a decoy – he's the boy
Boris Johnson's wig stunt double

Who can make no sense at all
And complicate this puzzle
Misdirect – and deflect …
Boris Johnson's wig stunt double

Here's the trick – need a prick
To try and burst this bubble?
He's the man – without a plan
Boris Johnson's wig stunt double

An extra man is needed
So from the bench the sub'll
Be instead – that talking head
Boris Johnson's wig stunt double

The real perpetraitor hides
Behind the party rubble
When it's time – for the firing line
Boris Johnson's wig stunt double

**There's No Truth In The Rumour That The Song Playing For
All Those People Was 'It's My Party And I'll Lie If I Want To'**
#697 / 13:01:2022

There'll be a thorough investigation
About this party situation
An enquiry, totally independent
While you try to appear repentant

Waiting for the evidence
If you were at your residence
At this particular juncture, you
Won't say exactly what is true

As far as you were honestly aware
Everybody was working there
Enjoying the lovely weather and thinking
Might as well get snacks and drink in

There really isn't that much in it
You just popped in for twenty minutes
Thanked the hundred in your garden
And now you want to beg our pardon?

Your email said bring your own booze
The Queen was alone with empty pews
You had a party while people were dying
Everyone knows that you are lying

Once so jolly and so affable
Now a joke that's sick and laughable
Lame excuses, so pathetic
You really do not seem to get it

How long to apologise?
Lies – lies – lies – lies – lies – lies – lies
Like those before didn't toe the line
Follow their lead – just resign

An Apology On Behalf Of The Poet
#698 / 14:01:2022

For any who read these words
And have been offended
I am here to apologise
And say … er
Sorry

But
In my defence
This was not a poem
But in fact a random selection of words
Written down during a business meeting
That have since been rearranged
To give the impression of a deliberate poem

Furthermore
These words have now been made public
And are here for all to see
But it is not a poem
Merely the written agenda, minutes
And possible shopping list for cheese and wine

In fact
I was only present at this meeting
Where the alleged poem was conceived
For a matter of minutes
Although in retrospect
I should have realised
That the people in my back bedroom
With pens and paper
Who I had forgotten I had invited
To bring their own prose
Were not just ignoring national guidelines
But having more fun than me
At my own residence

Nevertheless
Any resemblance to a poem
Is purely coincidental
And open to interpretation
Owing to some lines
Looking shorter
And the liberal literal use
Of a lot of alliteration

As this situation threatens to become verse
I would once again
Humbly apologise
But rest assured
I recognise

That evidence will be independently inspected
To ascertain if words selected
Followed sequences expected
With any images connected
Any similes collected
So if you have been affected
All these words will be dissected
No stone unturned or neglected
In case you have been misdirected

This is not a poem

Official Party Line
#699 / 15:01:2022

Cheese? Wine?
Working time
The official party line

Drinking, eating
Business meeting
Outdoor tables, casual seating

Top team
New routine
Wine day Friday, let off steam

Chin chin
Get them in
Down in one street, same again?

Bad taste?
Out of place?
More wine? On the case

Weekly date
Congregate
Everyone else can isolate

Getting longer
This list's wrong – a
Party line that is a conga

Cameras, candid
Double standard
Nobody yet reprimanded

On its way
The final say
They want fifty shades of Gray

Undermining
Jeers and whining
No crime seen – no resigning

Yet

Operation Save Big Dog
#700 / 16:01:2022

Recognising big, big trouble
The truth is going to the burst this bubble
Reinforcements at the double
Operation Save Big Dog

The party gate is open wide
He tries to isolate and hide
Everybody knows he lied
Operation Save Big Dog

He thinks that this is Hollywood
Believes it's all been jolly good
Did not think his folly would
Operation Save Big Dog

He wants to play the conquering hero
But been fiddling – just like Nero
His chances now – simply zero
Operation Save Big Dog

Believes it's all a jolly jape
Now he wants the mask and cape
Thinks he's in The Great Escape
Operation Save Big Dog

Thinks everything will be alright
Looking Gray but washing white
Fifty shades of Tory shite
Operation Save Big Dog

All the muck he has been raking
All the liberties he's taken
Still thinks he can save his bacon
Operation Save Big Dog

Number Ten last chance saloon
Deflating like a burst balloon
This party party's over soon
Operation Save Big Dog

Mission Improbable
#701 / 17:01:2022

Crass and crash course politician
The only course is now collision
Impossible to win this mission
Operation Save Big Dog

A captain who once thought un-droppable
Now his exit looks unstoppable
Hoping for mission improbable
Operation Save Big Dog

Broke the rules he put in place
He's a state of disgrace
No chance now of saving face
Operation Save Big Dog

Won't admit or take the blame
A man with no real plan again
Now he wants to vote remain
Operation Save Big Dog

Operation Save Big Dog?
What on earth's he thinking of?
Who would really want this job?
Operation Save Big Dog

Ignore extraneous paraphernalia
Just like the Ashes in Australia
This rescue mission – doomed to failure
Operation Save Big Dog

Let's Defund The BBC
#702 / 18:01:2022

In the land where speech is free
In this so-called democracy
Just because you don't agree
Let's defund the BBC

Because they will not bend their knee
And question your ability
Your only answer seems to be
Let's defund the BBC

Report your mediocrity
Or giving the third degree
Your response is your decree
Let's defund the BBC

Because you cannot referee
You review your policy
Proclaiming them the enemy
Let's defund the BBC

Defend impartiality?
Refund funds from PPE?
We're sick of your hyperbole
Let's defend the BBC

The programmes we all love to see
All the natural history
Sport and art and comedy
Let's defend the BBC

Not for your minority
But for the majority
Clarity and quality
Let's defend the BBC

Nobody Told Me
#703 / 19:01:2022

Because I am the Prime Minister
I should have been told
Of any potential rule breaking
Because not to do so
Would be to withhold crucial information
That could possibly damage my reputation
And make me look foolish
And that would be untenable
Because I am the Prime Minister

And because I am the Prime Minister
I should have been duly warned
That all this might come to light
But nobody told me about this possibility
And that is a dereliction of their duty
Because I am the Prime Minister

And as the Prime Minister
I should have been told
That should all this be made public
I would have to say
That nobody told me
I was breaking my own rules
But they did not tell me
So I did not know
And I should have known
Because I am the Prime Minister

But nobody told me
All these things that I knew
Nobody warned me
That it would make me look incompetent
Nobody told me
Nobody told me
Nobody told me
About
Operation Dead Meat

Hey Boris, Please Don't Go ...
#704 / 20:01:2022

Hey Boris, please don't go
Please stay, whatever you do
Carry on your carrying on
There's no-one quite as bad as you

Hey Boris, don't desert us
In this, our needy hour
The opposition has more chance
The longer time you are in power

Hey Boris, please just stay
Another year – or longer
'Cause if you go then we all know
The Tories will get stronger

Hey Boris, please don't sign
That resignation letter
As your party might recover
When they get someone much better

Hey Boris, please remain
We don't want you to exit
Just stay and get things done so well
Just like you did with all things Brexit

To See, You Have To Look Properly
#705 / 21:01:2022

I have seen no evidence
To substantiate the claim
That strong arm blackmail tactics
Are used and are to blame

But then again, I am the one
Who saw no evidence
Of cheese and wine and parties
At my home residence

Somebody Somewhere Must Be Tolling A Bell ...
#706 / 22:01:2022
for Meat Loaf

Like the T-rex dragon you were
You strode into the
Nineteen seventy-seven punk rock saloon
Looked at them squarely
Laughed, roared
Blew hell fire smoke in their faces
And carried on being you

Over the top and all over the place
Everything louder than everything else
Reclaiming all the clichés
And adding even more
Pantomime rock and roll opera
At its very best

Pantomime dinosaur
Rock and roll mammoth
Operatic behemoth
And then some
You knew it
You smiled
You didn't care
And for that, you were punk rock personified
You did it your way

My dad once turned off Whistle Test in disgust
During your 'Paradise by the Dashboard Light' antics
And I had to pretend I didn't really like you
While trying to explain that your name was "Meat"

Meat? Meat?!
As in Belly Pork?
Meat ... Loaf?
Like being called Pork Roll

Since then
You have always been around
And there's always a time for a song
That breaks down the barriers
And rolls back the years

You weren't my all-time favourite
But you always made me smile
And I always sang along
So I suppose
Two out of three ain't bad

And here we are, wishing that
Heaven might have waited a little bit longer

Instead, we'll look again at that cover art
And play that song as loud as we possibly can

"The sirens are screaming, the fires are howling
Way down in the valley tonight …"

In The Interests Of Political Balance
#707 / 23:01:2022

Imagine the furore
We'd all be absorbing
If all this corruption
Was Jeremy Corbyn?

Muslimness
#708 / 24:01:2022

Muslimness
Not something you want
Muslimness
Doesn't quite fit

Muslimness
Makes people uncomfortable
Muslimness
Whatever it is

Is exactly what you need

Beyond Redemption
#709 / 25:01:2022

Josephine, aged seven
Cancelled her birthday party
The Queen, likewise
Scales down a royal birthday
In line with national guidelines
Set by you

But not you
So what makes you so different?
Are you more important than young Josephine?
And Her Majesty The Queen?
Or do you just not care
And thought you wouldn't be found out?

Yet here you are, exposed
As the fraud many thought you already were
Was it all worth the cake?
Was it all worth the candles?
We are not in this together
At all

You have proved that
Time after time after time
And now it is your time
You are beyond redemption

Nothing To Report?
#710 / 26:01:2022

Waiting for the findings
Whatever they may say
Hoping that it's black and white
Not fifty shades of grey

Ambushed By A Cake
#711 / 27:01:2022

Ambushed by a cake you say? Surely some mistake
All of that security and ambushed by a cake?
Ambushed by a cake you say? Give the man a break
Who pays the price for one small slice – ambushed by a cake

Ambushed by a cake you say, ambushed by a cake
Taken by surprise as Colin the Caterpillar lay in wait
Cornered by some burning candles, icing and a flake
What's a man supposed to do when ambushed by a cake?

What possible evasive action could a person take?
Overpowered by sugar and flour … ambushed by a cake
Confronted with confectionary and no chance of escape
Surrender to that rocky road … ambushed by a cake

Battered by a Battenburg, trapped by a tray bake
Surrounded by Victoria sponge … ambushed by a cake
Tricked by triple chocolate chip, a simple slip to make
Hemmed in, undefended … ambushed by a cake

Given all the guideline and given what's at stake
Is that your best excuse … ambushed by a cake?

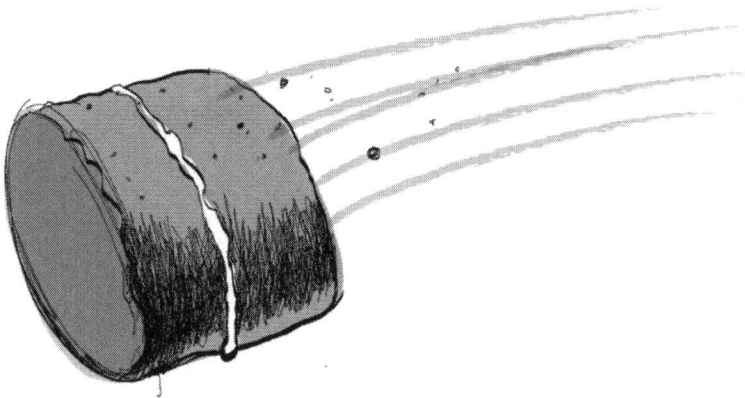

Green Bananas
#712 / 28:01:2022
for Barry Cryer

T'wit
Yorkshire for
A natural aptitude for using words and ideas
In a quick and inventive way to create humour

A perfect description of you
An insatiable passion for jokes and wordplay
No entendre ever undoubled
Not just wit and tomfoolery
But warmth, heart and above all else

A bringer of joy and laughter
Much more than a comedian
A sharer of light
And lifter of spirits

You worked with all the greats
And made them even greater
But you are one of the greats
Yet always humble

A natural encourager
Birthday phone calls and parrot gags
You have been here forever
You will be here forever

We will always think of you and smile
Thank you sir
Barry Cryer, we salute you
And in your honour

We are all off to put a parrot in the fridge
And buy a big bunch of green bananas
For you
The wit
And now it is indeed
Mournington Crescent

We Don't Really Need To Read Between The Lines
#713 / 29:01:2022

This is a totally independent poem
However, someone called Sue is my new
Editor and my publisher is called Cressida
Consequently, certain lines
█████ ████ ████
█ ██████████ █████████ ████
██ ███ ████ █ ███
████ and completely ████
Overall, the original heart of the poem is still
Visible, it's just that you ███ ███ it
█ ██ █ █
███ unsuitable █████ ██
█ ██ █████ ██ public consumption
Even the section concerning
████ ████ ██ ████ ███
████ █ █ ██ and
████ █ ██ ███
█ █ █ ████
Rendered ██ ████
██████ ███ █ totally inappropriate
Unsurprisingly, the bit about
████ ███ ██ ███ ███ █
███ █ ███ and you will never see
███ ██ █ ████
Properly █████ █ █ █ or that bit
Reading a poem where you can't see
Every single word is difficult and can
Prejudice the overall truth instead
Of finding out what
Really happened
Though I have learnt to write acrostically

**Your Supporters Say That's Time To
Put All This Behind You And Move On**
#714 / 30:01:2022

To be honest
You have a lot to put behind you

If you were a slug
The slime would trail for miles and miles and miles

Oh ... you are a slug
And it does

Christian Forgiveness
#715 / 31:01:2022

So
Mister Gove has called for
Christian forgiveness
To be honest
I'm all for it

However
The problem with forgiveness
Is that the sinner
First has to acknowledge their transgressions
Confess their guilt
And be truly sorry
Then repent and have a change of heart
Looking forward to that then

Like I said
Christian forgiveness
I'm all for it

Just Who Are You Trying To Kid?
#716 / 01:02:2022

There's no full report as yet
But we all know just what you did
We don't need to see those words
So just who are you trying to kid?
What you did was what you wanted
Things you did forbid
You know that we all know it
So just who are you trying to kid?
So Sue Gray might have her say
On secrets that you hid
It doesn't matter anyway
So just who are you trying to kid?
You might try and vet the Met
So that they don't lift the lid
No-one trusts you anymore
So just who are you trying to kid?
You writhe in all directions
A sly and slimy squid
But cannot wriggle out this time
So just who are you trying to kid?
How the mighty fall and squirm
And in the mire you slid …
Just how low will you go?
So just who are you trying to kid?
Delay – distract – distract – delay
One last futile bid
Even those who liked you don't
So just who are you trying to kid?
Time to face the music
Time to just get rid
Good riddance to bad rubbish
So just who are you trying to kid?
Way, way off the chart
Totally off the grid
It's not funny anymore
So just who are you trying to kid?

The Prime Minister In Waiting
#717 / 01:02:2022

Spoke with clarity, dignity
Empathy, honesty
Authority and power
Statesman-like and trustworthy

He communicated and connected
On behalf of the people
In short
He was and is
Everything you are not

**Just When We Think You Can't Stoop Any Lower
You Mention J*mmy S*v*l***
#718 / 02:02:2022

Every spiteful slur you stutter
Every lie you glibly mutter
With every single word you utter
You sink lower in the gutter
Finding your rightful place

So Many Reasons
#719 / 03:02:2022

As if there aren't enough reasons already
To mistrust your mismanagement
You then give us eight point four billion more
Eight point four billion
Eight Point Four Billion Pounds
Money that could build hospitals – but didn't
Money that could benefit the NHS – but hasn't
Money written off, wasted, gone
Which sums the whole lot of you up

Hypocrisy Seeps From Your Every Pore
#720 / 04:02:2022

Sending out supporters
Doesn't seem so sensible
Platitudes and attitudes
So incomprehensible
The mission is impossible
Defend the indefensible

It wasn't just the PM
Who was party to the party
All the hundred others
And assorted glitterati
Indifferent and ignorant
Happy, hale and hearty

So all you party goers
Where is your ability
To recognise and make a stand
And take responsibility
Collective and compliant
Your unreliability

A few are seeing through
The vacuous veneer
Day by day by day
A few more disappear
One question still remains
Why are you still here?

The Boy Stood On The Burning Deck
#721 / 05:02:2022

The boy stood on the burning deck
His hair was all a-quiver
He gave a cough
Couldn't give a toss
And sold us down the river

The boy stood on the burning deck
With pockets full of matches
That lit the candles
On the cake
But denied it in despatches

The boy stood on the burning deck
The flames grew ever higher
All because
He is and was
Liar liar LIAR

Days Like These
#722 / 06:02:2022

Yesterday was not a day for politics
But a day for football
The FA Cup and friendship

Chips and gravy, beer and banter
Goals and jubilation
Even the rain could not dampen the spirits

The rekindling of belief and the return of optimism
For just one day and we all look forward to
More days like this

Jubilee
#723 / 07:02:2022

Mum and dad always insisted
On watching The Queen's Speech
Three o'clock Christmas Day
Part of the routine
Part of our day

And while others around her
Fail and fall
Or simply pass away
She remains
Steadfast and true
Unmoving and dignified
Humble and honest
An example to us all

And for these reasons
I will raise a glass
And toast this jubilee
Ma'am

There Are Still Those Who Believe
In You And Your Lies
#724 / 08:02:2022

The slurs that you so glibly quipped
Angry crowds repeat as fact
Yet still you won't apologise
Redact or take them back

**Carry On Digging Boris, Hopefully The Hole
Will Be Big Enough To Bury You In**
#725 / 09:02:2022

Arrogant, aloof
Keep your social distance from
Decency and truth

Defiantly crass
Above all consequences
And laws that you pass

Ugliness and lies
Don't deviate at all and
Don't apologise

Nastiness you spout
The Bullingdon bully who
Continues to shout

Keep digging that hole
Thinking you're our country's heart
But really our soul

Brazen barefaced cheek
Flatulence and stench comes from
Ev'ry word you speak

Always Lewo, Never Arwel
#726 / 10:02:2022

Friends since the infants
We thought we'd be friends as pensioners
But life is a thieving bastard sometimes
Always Lewo, never Arwel
The customary addition on an "o" or a "y"
In order to necessitate a nickname
Them's the rules

You must have tired of the joke
At the start of every new school year
When a teacher would ask your name
Arwel
Pardon?
Arwel
What?
And then some wag would always say
Ah – well – never mind
As if it was the first time
But we can't say that now

Sat'days at the rec
The mecca when everyone had a bike
Jumpers for goalposts football
Borrowed bats and mismatched wickets for cricket
Even a DIY golf course
Thanks to bamboo canes, garden trowels
And random clubs
Innocence, simplicity and fun

Channelling your inner Reg Dwight
For the fifth form band Sliced Ice
Then Rick Wakeman, in a blazer not a cape
For sixth form concerts and beyond
And here we are

Or here we were
Over fifty years later
Still meeting up
Reliving those memories and more
The regular four

Lewo, Ammo, Wiggy, Cooky and Heatlumps
The latter being the exception to the nickname rule
And actually having a nickname longer than his surname

Listening to tales of days out at the cricket
Or your hairbrained schemes of truffle farming
But no more
Not now
Cheers Lewo
Thanks mate
We will raise a glass
When we three meet again
The first of our gang to go
Cheers Lewo
You never did find the truffles

I Said I Wouldn't Resort To Cheapness
Based Upon Her Unfortunate Surname ...
#727 / 11:02:2022

At last
A resignation

Yet we are all resigned
To it not being the one
That we all know it should be
She didn't fulfil her obligations
Related to her public office
And the standards therein

So
We have the withdrawal of a Dick
From active service

Alas, the wrong Dick
That dishonourable member
Is still standing
Oblivious and proud
Indecently exposed
Spouting rubbish
While shafting the rest of us

Friday Night Is Scunthorpe Night
#728 / 12:02:2022

I've never had a Friday night in Scunthorpe before
A place I can't think of without bringing to mind
A line of a Cooper Clarke poem that I can't repeat here

Yet here I am, last minute
Having only just seen that
Mark Steel is in town

Gloriously grumpy and swearily bemused
Ranting at stupidity, injustice
And anything else that springs to a random mind

Hilariously at odds with modern life
While acknowledging that the past was not better
And they weren't the good old days

Laughter, connection and more laughter
And after all, we were out
After all ... this, we were out

Together, with a bloke who felt like our mate
Warm, sharp, angry, baffled, rambling
And most of all, funny

Very funny indeed
As we, his ramshackle congregation
Celebrated this comic communion together

In a week when laughter was needed
We got it in Scunthorpe
On a Friday night

A Letter From The Met
#729 / 13:02:2022

Dear Sir
As we seek to establish the facts
Please complete this sheet and send it back
Answer truthfully, wherever you can
Then we can see just how things stand
We'll then assess all evidence
With customary due diligence
So you can answer easily
Multiple choice – a, b, c
We thought it simpler
If options were fewer
Answer Yes or No
Or Not Quite sure
So …
Is this a questionnaire?
Do you have stupid hair?
Are you the Prime Minister?
Are you hiding something sinister?
Do you like cheese or wine?
Did you have a quiz at Christmas-time?
Have you ever been ambushed by a cake?
Are you a lying, cheating snake?
Yes, Yes, Yes
No, Er … Yes
Not Quite Sure
A possibility at best
Absolutely, unequivocally, definitely
Under no circumstances NO NO NO
Thank you sir
Off you go

A Verse You'll Never Find
In A Card That's Never Made
#730 / 14:02:2022

For all those alone
Who can't find the spark
All of those shattered
Broken of heart

Those who are weakened
Lost to self-doubt
Don't want to stay in
But scared to go out

Those without love
Those who have lost
All those rejected
Counting the cost

All who feel distant
With nobody near
On this, the loneliest
Day of the year

No chocolates or roses
Or shared sparkling wine
This poem's for you
Sad Valentine

If It Looks Like Aggression
Then It Is Usually Aggression
#731 / 15:02:2022

Tanks on borders awaiting orders …
Routine operations?
Or a show of strength of their intent …
Imminent invasions?

Questions Brought, Answers Sought
#732 / 16:02:2022

Exotic resorts by all reports
Young escorts snapped and caught?
A prince of sorts, doesn't like courts
Innocence bought? Money talks

Not Happy, Not Glorious
#733 / 17:02:2022

If it's not one thing, it's another
Who would be a royal mother?
Scandal, shame, a total travesty
Sympathy for Her Majesty

**Today Is Not A Day For Ladders
Or Ill-Fitting Toupées**
#734 / 18:02:2022

Today is not a day for ladders
Ill-fitting toupées or tightrope walking

I think I'll give the abseiling
And the windsurfing a miss

I've long since lost my kite
But today it wouldn't be worth untangling

If we had any hatches
Today is a day for battening them down

Staying in with a good book, a hot cup of tea
And looking after the ones you love

Eunice Makes You Sound Like A Kindly Aunt
#735 / 19:02:2022

Monstrous waves, cauldron seas
Tumbling spires, crashing trees

Toppled lorries, ferries tossed
Cables whipped, power lost

Landing planes, bravely battled
Every fence and gatepost rattled

Unstoppable and untamed
Force of nature, strangely named

**And I Only Put The Last Two Words In
So That It Worked**
#736 / 20:02:2022

Looking at the rain
No desire to venture out
Strange then, that the best
I can come up with today
Is this cinquain … only just

The First Of Many More
#737 / 21:02:2022

No longer the dining room table
There is a new desk
Not brand new
But new to me

I have spent several amiable hours
Putting new legs on it
And playing jigsaws
With the furniture in the spare room
Getting rid of the old bed
So that I can actually sit at the desk

And get to the record player
And the numerous bookshelves
And still have space to display at least three prized ukuleles
While sitting in an armchair from downstairs
Admiring everything around me

Option two
Looking out of the front window
Is currently the best
So here I am
Pen in hand
Notebook spread out before me
Writing a new poem
At a new desk

Like I said
The desk is not brand new
Much like the poem
All these words have been used before
But here we are
Desk and words
Creating the new
And preparing for the future

We're All In This Together Then …
#738 / 22:02:2022

Self-isolation scrapped
Free tests axed
Treat it just like flu
Now it's over to you

It Shouldn't Matter But Somehow It Does
#739 / 23:02:2022

Sitting in a deserted hotel bar
And the TVs are on
Sound down
Often the best way when you are involved

I know you are talking about
The crisis in Ukraine
Impending possible war and catastrophe
But all I can think about is your hair

And you can't even take that seriously
Shallow, I know
And now I'm worried
That we have that quality in common

No Disputing, Mister Putin
#740 / 24:02:2022

When the tanks are pointed in one direction
The air strikes have started to hit their targets
And forty-five thousand body bags have been ordered
There is no going back

And all this from a man claiming to have launched
"A special military operation"
That is being conducted by "peacekeepers"

Not The Poem I Want To Write
#741 / 25:02:2022

I want to write about the smiles of children
Laughing at poems in school halls

I want to write about books and fun
The joy of an ordinary school day

But these are not ordinary days
These are days of horror

We are living in days that will be remembered
For all the wrong reasons

I do not want to write of war
But some things we cannot ignore

Power
#742 / 26:02:2022

Powerless … all we can do is pray
Powerful … all you can do is prey

The Communion Of Music
#743 / 27:02:2022

After all this time
Amidst all this negativity
We were ready

Ready to have our spirits lifted
Ready to join together with others
Ready to sing a new song

With friends old and new
We gathered in a darkened room
And celebrated the magic

Not with hymns and bread and wine
But guitars and pies and peas
This is the sign of our peace

Until the next time
Peace be with you, brothers and sisters
Peace be with us all

I May Be A Woolly Wishy-Washy Liberal Pacifist
With Idealistic Notions Of Peace And Love
But Today In Church ...
#744 / 28:02:2022

I thought about pure evil
And the power he's amassing
I prayed for peace and love
And a bloody good assassin

Today Is A Black Tie Day
#745 / 01:03:2022

My friend Ian sings of an old black tie
Today is one such day

The day we gather to say goodbye
Old school mates in black ties

Once, ill-fitting blazers and chunky knots
Today, well-worn suits and the thin black tie

And as we consider death face to face
We can't just think of our friend

We can't help but think of innocent others
Taken, oppressed and lost forever

But for now, in these moments today
We will think of our friend, Lewo

As we straighten our black ties
For these are the ties that bind

Cheers Lewo
Cheers mate

The Final Curtain
#746 / 02:03:2022

Last minute substitute
I was needed for one last task
To carry you that short journey
From hearse to resting place
Together, with friends and family
We shared your burden
One last act of friendship
Before the final curtain
All we carry now are the memories
And long they will live

Every Day Is Book Day
#747 / 03:03:2022

For some of us
Every day is book day

On this world book day
We remember one of our own

One on her own
One of the true greats

Not a blazer of trails or setter of trends
Just a purveyor of eternal quality

Pictures and stories, universally loved
That spanned generations

She captured our childhoods perfectly
And also our children

They have lived on
They will live on again and again

From once upon a time
To happy ever after

Thank you Shirley Hughes
Thank you so much, for so much

Surely Some Sort Of Mistake?
#748 / 04:03:2022

So, you are now a sir – for what exactly?
A nobody who is now a knight of the realm

Is there anything during your public duty
That you have done particularly well?

Nothing springs to mind, nothing at all
Arise Sir Gavin … wrong on so many levels

**In The Midst Of War It Feels Somewhat Trite
To Write A Poem About A Cricketer**
#749 / 05:03:2022
for Shane Warne

The king of spin
Revolution at your fingertips
Bamboozler of batsmen
Entranced and hypnotised
By your ever-expanding web of deception
Trapped by your threads of trickery
Bursting onto the scene with the impossible
The ball of the century
Jiggery pokery hocus pocus magic
Hollywood bowler, box office great
Nothing quite ever as it seams
Surprising and confusing
Where
                              anything
                                                            could
                                                                          happen
each
                    ball
and often
did

Eternity Is Too Short A Time For You To Suffer
#750 / 06:03:2022

Vladimir
When you get to hell
As you surely will
Be sure
To compare notes
With Adolf
As you play
Despot Top Trumps
And may the flames of your sins
Burn forever and ever
And ever
Amen

Act Of War
#751 / 07:03:2022

Your actions will be seen
As an act of war
Consequences which
Never seen before

Your actions represent
An act of war
To which we will respond
With even more

Special operations
Our special reasons for
Our course which is not
An act of war

Truth
#752 / 08:03:2022

They say that truth
Is the first casualty of war
Maybe in Russia
But not for the rest of the world

For the first time in history
We are seeing front line reporting
Ordinary journalists
Extra-ordinary journalism

Everyday refugees with mobile phones
Documentaries of death and destruction
Uploading their truth to Twitter
Facing the facts on Facebook

We can see evil for what it is
Unfiltered
Unedited
A war zone on a mobile phone

And the truth is hard to watch
These are not extras in movies
But families in peril
And with this truth

No-one need be ignorant
No-one should have an excuse
To do nothing
With truth comes responsibility

"Spot on." *John Wat Tyler Parton*

Pleas
#753 / 09:03:2022

Please please
In days like these
Vis-à-vis the refugees
Release the need for visas
Please

Tankas And Tanks
#754 / 10:03:2022

The man who would be
Churchill but is not listens
To the man who wants
Not his Churchill moment but
Has to be right now

While the man who would
Be king bombs hospitals and
Civilians then
Targets women, children as
Evil terror strikes once more

Hiding
#755 / 11:03:2022

Today I hid
Hid from the war
Hid from the destruction
Hid from the devastation
I had other things to do
A world away
There are those millions
Wishing they could hide too
Wishing they had other things to do

Blackbird In The Living Room
#756 / 12:03:2022

High winds, a chimney
And a blackbird in the living room
Not a good combination
A fluttering mess of panic and confusion
And that was just us

Too fast, too furious
The cardboard boxes were never going to work
Neither were the dust sheets over the banister
To create a curtain of safety
And corridor of opportunity
With all doors wide open
To the afternoon rain

In the end
It was a carefully thrown tablecloth
Behind a corner unit that did the trick
That, and a snow shovel underneath
Trying to scoop the living feathery bundle
Off the carpet and at arm's length
Outside onto the front garden

My arm's length, it has to be said
I was at the safer end of the proceedings
Pretending I knew what I was doing
My wife, meanwhile
Directed things at the business messy end
We called it teamwork
But it wasn't really
My wife, the superhero

Someone once made a film called *Snakes on a Plane*
We've had *Blackbird in the Lounge*
It could have been worse ... *Buzzard in the Bathroom*
Magpie in a Mini, Seagull in a Sidecar
Or even worse ... *Parrot in a Phone Box*

Sunday Morning Haiku
#757 / 13:03:2022

Music with my friends
Plus Methodist cottage pie
Top Saturday night

Perspective And Hope
#758 / 14:03:2022

To be honest
Everton disappointed me
Yet again

I should be used to it by now
But you hope …
Usually against hope

Now getting seriously worried
Can't see where the next win
Will come from

Dangerously close to relegation
Although it's not really
Actual danger though, is it?

I mean, nobody has died
Left their homes and cities
Because of bombs and tanks

Perspective
We all need perspective and hope
Apparently, we have got games in hand

The Man Who Won't Back Down
#759 / 15:03:2022

He's the man who will not change
The man who won't turn round
The man who's gone too far
The man who won't back down

The man who will not listen
The man who takes more ground
The man with too much power
The man who won't back down

The man who would be king
The king with armoured crown
The man with an iron fist
The man who won't back down

His currency is bloodshed
His call a death-knell sound
His legacy is slaughter
The man who won't back down

Just Another Day
#760 / 16:03:2022

Bombardment and bombs
Missiles and mayhem
Bullets and bandages
Hospitals and hostages

Disgust and disbelief
Horror and helplessness
Destruction and displacement
Innocents and invasion

At Last
#761 / 17:03:2022

A little good news
Well, a lot of good news
For family and friends

After all this time
Six long years
Freedom is a taste to be savoured

Incarceration and innocence
Vigil and patience
Justice at last

At least one family
Will celebrate being together tonight
Amidst the tears of joy

And not before time

I Know ...
#762 / 18:03:2022

I know there's a war going on
But tonight
My head was filled with football
Just football
The all-consuming importance
The vitality and necessity of winning
Or, at the very least, not losing
Genuinely nervous

Not quite squeaky whatever time
But pretty close
Clichéd but true
The drama and rollercoaster ride
When the referee conspires against us
One man down
And the fight against the odds
The elation of scoring deep, deep, deep
Into added time

And the eternity of the last few minutes
Before the total relief
Of the final whistle

Like I said
Not life or death at all
But somehow important all the same
I know ...

Lies And Missiles
#763 / 19:03:2022

The lies shoot
From your murderous mouth
As easily as the missiles fly
From your murderous machines

Reminder
#764 / 20:03:2022

Thank you, Mister Johnson
For reminding us

While we have been distracted
By the horrors of war and invasion
We had forgotten about you

Mister Zelenskyy
Is standing up for justice
The freedom of his people
Against the tyranny of evil

Mister Zelenskyy
Is standing side by side
With his ordinary extraordinary people
Defending their country
And their freedom
With their very lives

And you
You, Prime Minister
Have the temerity to compare

Their freedom fighting with Brexit ...
So thank you Prime Minister
For reminding us just how out of depth
And out of touch you really are

For reminding us of your non-existent grasp on real life
For reminding us that every stage
Is one for your personal opportunity
And for reminding us of the meanings of the words
Incompetent, embarrassing and untrustworthy

Usually
#765 / 21:03:2022

Usually
A middle-aged overweight man
In ill-fitting mis-matched attire
Trying to jog on a lonely beach
Would get my respect

But somehow
In your case I'll make an exception

One Head Of State Writes To Another
#766 / 22:03:2022

Thank you, Mister Putin
For the war that you have started
You've saved my job, they all forgot
How much I drank and partied

Two Lines About The Two Lines
#767 / 23:03:2022

Ironic, that after two years of writing about it
The two lines stare back and the truth is indisputable

Eco Worrier
#768 / 24:03:2022

You ask what symptoms I have got
Mass production – A-grade snot
In large industrial quantiteez
When I blow my nose or sneeze
A miserable man and his mucus macheen
Totally and completely green
Just imagine the situation
Had I not had the vaccination

You Draw The Lines
And We'll Read Between Them
#769 / 25:03:2022

In these trying times it's imperative we must
Be absolutely certain who to trust

A man who smirks through talk of refugees
Is definitely not one of these

Or a rich man who fails to use his powers
To help the poor in this land of ours

Just Another Statistic?
#770 / 26:03:2022

Cases climb by a million this week
According to reports

For once, I'm a number
A millionth of those statistics

And if I'm a living breathing statistic
Then that must mean that there are …

Nine hundred ninety-nine thousand
Nine hundred and ninety-nine

Other living breathing statistics
Let's hope and pray it stays that way

Today Might Be Mothering Sunday
But Mothers Are Mothers Every Day
#771 / 27:03:2022

Mothers of sons took flight
Sons of mothers stayed to fight
And when all this is over
We pray they all will reunite

Oh No! Crow!
#772 / 28:03:2022

The clatter in the living room
Was not my wife sorting the shutters
But a bird in the living room … again

Not a sparrow or blackbird this time
But a crow, the devil's own
What a carrion

History repeating but bigger and blacker
And crowier … which isn't a word
But is now

Down the chimney – again
Black cacophony of chaos – again
The hearth needs a good hoovering

As does the carpet and the arm of the sofa
Will never be the same shade again
The dustsheets almost did the job

But almost is almost
And amid the rapid flutter to the shutters
We retreated, doors open, wide open

And, as easy as one, two, three
Out it went, drawn by the light and blue skies
We closed the door quickly

After the crow flies, cleaning up … again
We don't want this to happen … again
Two dust sheets and a tablecloth our answer

Wedged up the hole in the chimney
The crow will not enter this way again
Neither will Santa Claus now

And The Winner Is ... No-One
#773 / 29:03:2022

Two wrongs will never ever make a right
But they'll always make headlines on Oscar night

The Results Are In
But Don't Hold Your Breath
If You're Waiting For Justice
#774 / 30:03:2022

The police confirmed the crimes today
The police confirmed the fines today
What's unconfirmed
And still to learn
Is who will go and who will stay

Although I think we all know anyway

So Here's An Idea,
It Won't Make Things Alright But ...
#775 / 31:03:2022

What if Michelle Mone
And PPE Medro
Used their profits of up to
Seventy-six million pounds
(Yes, million and yes, profit
And yes, selling to the NHS
In a time of national crisis
But let's not get into that right now)

So, what if they used their profits
To fund free testing kits for everyone?

April Fools?
#776 / 01:04:2022

The PM tells the truth and resigns there on the spot
The chancellor reneges, gives the poor all he has got
Tory cronies pay back profits from all the PPE
Nurses pay to park their cars while MPs park for free

Elvis lives in Rotherham and works in B&Q
He rides to work on Shergar on a saddle made for two
Lord Lucan's riding pillion and works on checkout three
Nurses pay to park their cars while MPs park for free

COVID is a fabrication and did not exist
A royal paid a fortune to someone he'd never kissed
Donald's trump means gas for all for all eternity
Nurses pay to park their cars while MPs park for free

There's a yeti in the White House who keeps on disappearing
A monkey with a banjo writing songs for Ed Sheeran
The monster from Loch Ness has a chat show on TV
Nurses pay to park their cars while MPs park for free

Liberace was a rock god and a raving crumpeteer
Drove all the ladies crazy with guitars and cigs and beer
There's an alien in the Kremlin who runs the KGB
Nurses pay to park their cars while MPs park for free

Jacob, Rees and Mogg are a wrestling tag team
Top hat, canes and cape, they're nasty and they're mean
Kings of the ring in WWE
Nurses pay to park their cars while MPs park for free

April Fools and jokes and japes, all a jolly wheeze
Only someone silly could believe in all of these
Yet one of them is true and is starting from today
MPs park for free while nurses have to pay

April Fools Day Was Yesterday
And Still The Fools Are In Charge
#777 / 02:04:2022

April Fools Day was yesterday
The day when COVID case numbers were the highest
And also the day when Free Universal Tests came to an end
Really? You couldn't make it up

Another Shining Example Of Us
All Being In This Together
#778 / 03:04:2022

In a show of solidarity with the population
As he seeks to level up, Rishi has gone on holiday
To his twelfth house in California
While not talking about his wife's £490 million shared
In a Russian-based company
So everything's alright then
We all know where we stand

Alone

This Is What You Voted For
#779 / 04:04:2022

As we look ahead to colder weather
It's good to know we're in this together
Heating allowances for MPs
While others starve and freeze

Don't Believe Your Eyes
#780 / 05:04:2022

Tower blocks, slowly smoking
Twisted buildings, girders poking
It's okay, only joking
All of it – fake news

City centre decimation
Destruction, death and devastation
Evidence of excavation
All of it – fake news

Tracks of tanks in dried up mud
Charred remains of bricks and wood
Where a hospital once stood
All of it – fake news

Upturned lorries, scattered load
Craters in a city road
From where the bombs and shells explode
All of it – fake news

Battered buildings, tattered flags
Massed graves and bloodstained rags
Burnt out cars and body bags
All of it – fake news

So sorry to burst your bubble
Someone's gone to a lot of trouble
Rearranging all that rubble
All of it – fake news

Abandoned shoe, an open case
Every detail, just in place
A movie scene of human waste
All of it – fake news

Don't believe your western eyes
Everything is civilised
Don't believe these Russian lies
All of it – fake news

Propaganda – see these signs
Read between the Russian lines
Recognise them as war crime
None of it – fake news

**You Will Be Spoken Of In The Same Breath
In Years To Come**
#781 / 06:04:2022

Deliberation and invasion
Devastation, degradation
Obliteration of a nation
Genocidal cultivation
Atrocities you ordered and allowed
Well … Hitler would be proud

Absolute control demander
You're the master and commander
Of creating national anger
Poisoned minds and propaganda
It doesn't become truth because you shout it loud
Well … Hitler would be proud

Attack! Attack! Attack! Attack!
Too far gone – no turning back
Tunnel vision, bloodstained track
Ears of stone, heart that's black
This, the evil furrow you have ploughed
Well … Hitler would be proud

Lines
#782 / 07:04:2022

The lines on your face tell their own story
Deep and permanent
All this has left its mark

We know parts of the narrative
But cannot read between your lines
Etched in skin forever

Wrinkled tattoos of furrowed pressure
The lines have been drawn
The battle lines on your face tell their own story

And it isn't once upon a time
And it won't be happy ever after
Just War and Peace

Without the peace

Hypothetically Speaking
#783 / 08:04:2022

Let's just imagine
That I am, perhaps, a public figure
And have £100,000 to spare
And wanted to appear charitable

I wouldn't give to
Say, a boarding school
In somewhere like Winchester
But more other deserving causes

Perhaps a food bank
A hospital, a care home
Maybe a children's charity
If only to give the impression that I cared

But I'm not a public figure
With wealth and privilege to spare
And those that are and have
Can spend their money just how they wish

It's theirs
But where they put their money
Shows just how much they care
Or not

So, it's all hypothetical really
Oh – and one more thing
If all the above were true
I'd make sure my wife paid her tax as well

They Were Not
#784 / 09:04:2022

They were not soldiers
Fighting on the front lines

But ordinary people
Fleeing on the railway lines

They were not fighters
Resisting your invasion

But woman and children
Trying to find safety

They were not attacking
Marching ever forward

But looking to retreat and hide
Searching for that solace

They were not advancing
Seeking to gain territory

But families displaced
Escaping from your carnage

They were not armed
But suitcases and carrier bags

A fcw gathered belongings
Hoping for a home that's new

They were not a threat at all
No danger to your forces

Yet still you pressed that button
Blowing them to smithereens

More signs
War times
Your crimes

When Boris Met Volodymyr
#785 / 10:04:2022

A man of honour and a man of trust
A man of principle and a man of action
A man of honesty and a man of grace
A man of the people and a man of example
A man of the moment and a man of greatness
And then there was the other one – the man in the ill-fitting suit

Helen Steiner Rice's Job Is Safe
#786 / 11:04:2022

Today is my wife's birthday
And we are away

A lovely hotel
Have eaten well
And will do so again later

Tomorrow too
Peaceful and relaxed
This is not the verse
That was in the card

There wasn't one
Instead
I wrote a few private words

And then these too
Which I will then make public
Once I've got the okay from Mrs C

And no
This wasn't her present
I will buy that from a garage forecourt later

P.S. It's not a car

It's Not A Very High Bar
But Still They Manage To Stoop Lower
#787 / 12:04:2022

The Conservatives all thank the Lord
Because of Nadine Dorries
They've found someone more useless
And stupider than Boris

To Be Honest,
Today's Wordle Is Very Easy
#788 / 13:04:2022

L	I	A	R	S
L	I	A	R	S
L	I	A	R	S
L	I	A	R	S
L	I	A	R	S

All You Decent Conservatives
#789 / 14:04:2022

All you decent Conservatives
There must be some of you, somewhere
Where are you?
Your silence is deafening

Surely you are embarrassed
Surely you are angry
Surely you want better ...
So, say so

You can't all be unwavering
Brown nosing, arse licking
Supporters of a charlatan liar
So, say so

Surely some of you are disappointed
And want much better for everyone
Surely you can see why so many
Are angry, bitter and feel totally let down

Your silence is deafening
Your lack of outrage is collusion
Your acceptance of moral failure
Is an acceptance of your own impotence

We all deserve so much better
And your willingness to accept incompetence
Indicates your own lack of decency
Compounding all the clichés

All the clichés about being out of touch
All the clichés about privilege
All the clichés about being uncaring
And one rule for some

Yet you tell us to move on
There are bigger issues to face
There are no bigger issues
Than trust and accountability

When you move on
Then so will we

The Hammer
#790 / 15:04:2022

The kiss and betrayal
The lies and the trial
The kangaroo court
A best friend's denial

The shout for Barabbas
The taunts and the jeers
The baying for blood
Where once there were cheers

The splinter of bones
The puncture of skin
The hammer that hammers
The nails further in

The washing of hands
The scathing and scorn
The stripping and whipping
The crown and the thorns

The cross that is carried
The wrists that are tied
The wine that is sour
The spear in the side

A thief on the left
A thief on the right
Forgiveness in death
Darkness and light

The sky turns to black
The thunder that breaks
The curtain that's torn
The earthquake that shakes

It – is – finished!
Uttered and cried
The final three words
The God that has died

The tomb and the angel
The breaking of day
The women arrive
The stone rolled away

Rife
#791 / 16:04:2022

The germs are still here
The infection still spreads
Ruining lives
Creating chaos and fear

COVID-19?
Omicron?
No
The Conservative Government

Sun Rise
#792 / 17:04:2022

For some of us, the
Rising sun on Easter Day
Is significant

An old day has died
Yet a brand new day begins
New start, even hope

Easter all year round
Resurrection each new day
The Son arises

Rwanda?
#793 / 18:04:2022

What? What? What the ... what?
Is this the answer you have got?
Out of sight and left to rot
Proves that you have lost the plot
Confusion and disbelief
Can quickly turn to anger
I'm not sure of the question
If the answer is Rwanda

Of all the possibles explored
Weighing risks against reward
An action that cannot be ignored
At very best, severely flawed
Is it just distraction
And Tory propaganda?
I'm not sure of the question
If the answer is Rwanda

"Our compassion may be limitless
Our capacity to help is not"
Not a hint of irony
In our PM's opening shot
And when our own Archbishop
Disagrees and will not pander
I'm not sure of the question
If the answer is Rwanda

The Archbishop Of Canterbury
Is Not The Archbishop Of Ranterbury
#794 / 19:04:2022

To shout out loud, so uncontrolled
In an angry noisy way
Declaiming and exclaiming
Vehement in what you say
Often silly or confused
Extreme views to implant
Not measured, calm and well thought out
Justin Welby does not rant

A message from a pulpit
A viewpoint based on grace
Quiet words, but honest words
Prescient in time and place
Define a rant and look again
Your evidence is scant
The irony of your response
Justin Welby does not rant

The outrage of the tabloids
The outcry from MPs
Their righteous indignation
Because he disagrees
Because he begs to differ
Not fit their skewered slant
He's branded and attacked
Justin Welby does not rant

A quiet man of God
Words seeking to be wise
Searching for the truth
Amidst the dirt and lies
Seeking to redress
All the poison that you plant
An Easter Sunday sermon
Justin Welby does not rant

Take the speck from your eyes first
Judge not that you be judged
If you're sinless cast the stone
Yet still you won't be budged
At least his words make sense unlike
Michael Fabricant
So carry on Archbishop
Justin Welby does not rant

This Is Not A Poem
#795 / 20:04:2022

I humbly apologise
But when I started this sequence of words
I did not realise it would become a poem
Even though, I am, indeed, a poet

And indeed, I do write poems
Yes, I picked up the pen
Yes, I found paper and began to write
But even then, it did not cross my mind

That this course of action may indeed
Lead to poetry
Not once during this time
Did I actually think about rhyme

I simply did not think it might
Turn to poetry as I write
It may sound crazy and absurd
Given that I write the words

Neither did it occur to me
That some may not want poetry
Ambushed by these words instead
Sorry if you feel misled

The pen and paper, my mistake
Like a birthday leads to party cake
Coincidence it tuned to verse
A failing on my part
For which I now say sorry
From the bottom of my heart
Innocent and unaware
Totally unknowing

Not my true intention
To write another poem
Honestly, I did not know
Where all of this was going

I did not think that this
Was yet another poem
Truth be told
I am a poet

And yet this time
I didn't know it
And so I take this time to
Sincerely apologise

And trust you that you will not choose
To read between my lies

Er ... lines

The Hole Truth
#796 / 21:04:2022

I have a spade
And it appears that I am digging a hole

The amount of dirt around me
May give the impression
That the hole is getting bigger
And yet it is not a hole

It may look like a hole
But despite its appearance
It is not a hole
And even if it is
Or could be
It is not a deliberate hole
It is merely that I have a spade
That keeps on digging

But it is not a hole
And that is the truth
The hole truth
And nothing but

Later
I will be using some whitewash
On a fence that I am building
Around the hole
That doesn't exist

Just What Could The Reason Be?
#797 / 22:04:2022

The House, not quite as common
Something different in the air
Why the change of atmosphere?
Ah yes … you wasn't there

Spring Is In The Air
#798 / 23:04:2022

I promised you a poem a day
So here's my daily verse
But I'm tired of writing poems
As the world is getting worse

I've decided now to channel
Helen Steiner Rice
So today, it's all cliché
And everything that's nice

Spring is in the air
Blossoms decorate the trees
A host of golden daffodils
Are dancing in the breeze

Fluffy lambs are gambolling
Whatever that may mean
Butterflies are fluttering
Tulips kiss from shoots of green

Bluebells bob, snowdrops sway
Birds, they nest and sing
A bit more sunshine every now
Now that it is Spring

Nature thrives and comes alive
My poems to inspire
But Putin's still a murderer
And Boris still a liar

Fats Waller And My Mother
#799 / 24:04:2022

In the car with mum
A repeated Desert Island Discs on the radio
And a choice by Humphrey Littleton
And out of the blue
Mum is singing along to Fats Waller

Er … Fats Waller?!
She harmonises the phrase

"It's a sin to tell a lie"
Pitch perfect and totally in time
Then tells me
"He could play, that one
You always remember the good songs
We always had the radio on in the background"

I don't think I've ever seen her dance
Ever
But she must have done at some point
Maybe around the house
When the radio was on in the background
Perhaps to Fats Waller

Before today
I'd have staked my house
That she'd no idea who he was

Mum, nearly ninety
And still surprising us

Really?
#800 / 25:04:2022

The Sharon Stone of politics
Can't anyone restrain her?
Distraction tactics of
The legs of Angela Rayner

Basic instinct is disgust
At the Daily Mail proclaimer
Trying to distract us with
The legs of Angela Rayner

Misogyny alive and well
From a certified no brainer
Whose choice is concentration on
The legs of Angela Rayner

Hear! Hear!
#801 / 26:04:2022

"Appalling, sexist, misogynistic tripe"
At last
Talking about a subject
He actually knows something about

From someone distracted by
Semi-naked women
Playing beach volleyball and
Glistening like wet otters

**It Doesn't Help When Your Name Sounds Like
A Seventies Brand Of Cheap Aftershave**
#802 / 27:04:2022

You could change the world forever
End poverty for the many
More money than common sense
As you don't seem to have any
All the good that you could do
For the many, not the few
A forty-four-billion-dollar hitter
And yet you choose to buy up Twitter
So I don't think I can trust
Someone like Elon Musk

Entrepreneur, investor
But the dreams you like to chase
Revolutionary transport
From earth to outer space
All that power, all that wealth
Could be used for the good of our health
A forty-four-billion-dollar hitter
And yet you choose to buy up Twitter
So I don't think I can trust
Someone like Elon Musk

Privilege and power
Should have a connection
To great responsibility
Yet you seem an exception
Yes, your money, yes, your views
You can spend it as you choose
A forty-four-billion-dollar hitter
And yet you choose to buy up Twitter
So I don't think I can trust
Someone like Elon Musk

Another Sordid Story
#803 / 28:04:2022

There's scandal in the Commons
That no-one can dispute
Shock on the front benches
The House of disrepute
It's a general election
His majority has grown
For the upstanding member
Watching porn on his mobile phone

Not paying full attention
To affairs of state
But somehow he's distracted
In a mass debate
His only contribution
A little groan or moan
From the upstanding member
Watching porn on his mobile phone

Dirty tricks and frontline whips
And that's just on his screen
Aye ayes to the left and right
At the sights that can be seen
Corruption and disruption
The seeds that you have sown
From the upstanding member
Watching porn on his mobile phone

Principles rise up then fall
Another sordid story
Misogyny, pornography
Another sordid Tory
Lascivious, oblivious
To any standards shown
For the upstanding member
Watching porn on his mobile phone

Behaviour that's despicable
Continues undeterred
We only hope his actions
Aren't louder than his words

And hoping that contention
Isn't the only bone
For the upstanding member
Watching porn on his mobile phone

A Psalm Of Balm
#804 / 29:04:2022

In the light of recent events
And this sordid revelation
This poem is an air freshener
To aid with fumigation

As things sink ever lower
With every passing motion
This poem is a wet wipe
Soaked in cleansing lotion

The guilty stench from off the bench
With each new revelation
This poem is needle
To aid inoculation

This poem is a wholesome balm
Think love and friendship, things like these
This poem is an antidote
To all the dirt and sleaze

Better Luck Next Time
#805 / 30:04:2022

At last it seemed that good sense had prevailed
When reading the headlines that said "Boris Jailed"
On further inspection, however, the menace
Was not the PM but the one who played tennis

As Excuses Go, It's Laughable
But Everyone Knows You're Lying Anyway
#806 / 01:05:2022

The fact of the matter
I was googling tractors
Didn't know the setting my server's on

Mistakenly picked on
Stupidly clicked on
A website that said "Massive Fergusons"

A Statement On Behalf Of
The Upstanding Member
#807 / 02:05:2022

Please take into consideration
This mitigating factor
I was looking for my wife …
She needed something to attract her

Just My Luck
#808 / 03:05:2022

A single magpie on the lawn
Always one for sorrow
I'm not superstitious
But I hope there's two tomorrow

At Least The Buses Are Heated
#809 / 04:05:2022

Living's getting costly
As fuel prices rise
People's lives are changing
Before our very eyes
One hot daily meal
And the other thing she does ...
Elsie's keeping warm on the bus

Numbers I can't even say
Are profits by BP
So somebody has done okay
As far as I can see
And if that's true then why not do
Something new because
Elsie's keeping warm on the bus

Who is going to make a stand?
Who is going to act?
Who is going to take in hand
This debilitating fact?
No-one wants to call it out
So who will make a fuss
While Elsie's keeping warm on the bus?

It may seem obvious and crass
But it's worth repeating
MPs with allowances
For residential heating
It seems a cliché when we say
There's them and then there's us
But Elsie's keeping warm on a bus!

Millions of Elsies
Millions are struggling
Millions are worrying
As bills are more than doubling
Neglected now by those elected
In whom we put our trust

So, Elsie's keeping warm on the bus
Albert's keeping warm on the bus
Nanna's keeping warm on the bus
Grandad's keeping warm on the bus

Unreal Madrid
#810 / 05:05:2022

Not a shot on target for eighty-nine minutes
Two goals down on aggregate
We thought it was all over
Then out of nowhere
Bang!
Bang!
Then bang again
Wow

Like a fighter on the ropes
Beaten but not quite down and out
Three sucker punches
And the unthinkable was real

Breath-taking drama
Savage plot twists
Football as theatre
The magic of sport
Where anything can happen
But usually doesn't

Funny old game
Unbelievable Jeff

When I Say "Right" I Obviously Mean "Correct"
#811 / 06:05:2022

Seats lost
Local election
At least it's a step
In the right direction

Not Very Long Ago It Was ...
#812 / 07:05:2022

Time to move on
There's nothing to see
There are greater issues to cause us worry

Yet ... somehow now
It's different here
With beer for Keir and take away curry

Yesterday's Headlines –
Almost Right
#813 / 08:05:2022

The Daily Express led with
"Bullish Boris Back On Track"

I didn't realise the first word
Was an anagram

With a missing "t"

Number Four In The Charts
#814 / 09:05:2022

I'm number 4 in the charts
Sorry
We are number 4 in the charts
We being Don Powell's Occasional Flames
Don, Les, Martin and me
Not so much a boy band
More the flab four ...
Well, in my case anyway

Our little song is getting bigger
Thanks to you
Friends and fans keep on voting
27
20
14
10
And now ... 4

Not bad eh?
Never been number 4
For anything before
Stuck in the middle of
Tony Hadley and Mickey Dolenz
Above Marillion, Bryan Ferry
The Buzzcocks and Pink Floyd
And just behind Toyah
Not bad company, eh?

Not Bad Company
They are nowhere to be seen
They are not number 4
We are

Thanks to you, friends
Voted by you pop pickers

Any chance of number 1 next week?

A Matter Of Honour Or You're A Goner
#815 / 10:05:2022

Fine?
Resign
Integrity
Defined

Speech?
#816 / 11:05:2022

I looked but only saw her crown
Slightly out of Charles' reach
No royal fruit, perfect and round
No sign of The Queen's Peach

Red Ribbon Cutting And Photo Opportunities
#817 / 12:05:2022

A day of jubilation
And a cause of celebration
A way of giving all a vote of thanks

Like opening an exhibition
But surely not the acquisition
Addition and provision of food banks

Johnson's Rovers 100 – Starmer's Academicals 1
(Although the one is being double-checked by VAR)
#818 / 13:05:2022

So …
an ode to something like …
er …
The Daily Mail and The Daily Express perhaps …

Wherefore is your outrage now?
Wherefore your disgust?
Wherefore is your anger
At this lack of trust?

Wherefore art your standards?
Wherefore your morality?
Wherefore now your principles?
Wherefore your integrity?

Wherefore now your judgement?
Wherefore is your rage?
Wherefore is your righteousness?
Not on your front page

And so we wait and wait and wait
And wait some more, what for?
As based on previous bias
We'll wait for evermore

Marching On
#819 / 14:03:2022
for Mike Peters and The Alarm

I'd forgotten just how many words I knew
These anthems of my youth
From when I needed you
Really needed music

When music meant everything
And your work spoke a truth
Connected and declared, arms outstretched
Heart and meaning, dreams and hopes

That declaration, bold and brave
A clarion call that has never dimmed
Never lost its sheen
Never lost its power and potency

Still a watermark by which to judge
Everything else you've ever done
Still my favourite songs
And every emotion they hold

I don't need new music like once I did
I've got all the bands I've ever wanted
All the bands I've ever needed
The ones that were mine

Mine when I really needed them
The ones that filled the hole
Before love, children and family
Took their rightful places

But as a clichéd song once said
Music is my first love …
And tonight, your songs proved just that
I am still in love and I am still marching on

And now, I pray
We all pray
That it won't be long
Before you are marching on again too

Colours
#820 / 14:05:2022

In 1970
The burning playground question was
Who do you want to win the FA Cup Final
Leeds or Chelsea?
Living in Lancashire
The common bond was the north
Even though it was Yorkshire
You can't support the south
My nine-year-old logic was different
Everton played in blue
Chelsea play in blue
Therefore I wanted Chelsea to win
I still support Everton
Chelsea still play in blue
They are playing Liverpool
So ...

Actually, to be honest
I'm not as bothered as I once was
It may be the FA Cup
But it's just not the same anymore

Merseyside
#821 / 15:05:2022

I'm here on Merseyside
Certainly not to join in any FA Cup celebrations
And, much as I'd love to
Not to support the Blues in their fight for survival
Which could be confirmed mathematically
Should results go the right way
But here to support my daughter
Who is doing the half marathon at Aintree Racecourse
Go Daisy!
Four laps, hopefully no fences, you can do it
(And then I'll cheer for Everton later)

A Eurovision Poem On Cup Final Day ...
Mixing My Metaphors
#822 / 16:05:2022

I didn't recognise the football shirts
I didn't know the kits
The sequins and the shimmer
The glamour and the glitz
Sam Ryder – right on target
Almost made the top
Didn't we do well in the Eurovision Cup?

It didn't go to penalties
Or to VAR
Catch the song of the day
With this year's superstar
We came from last year's losers
To this year's runners up
Didn't we do well in the Eurovision Cup?

Aiming to be number one
Aiming for that goal
A bit of fancy footwork
A bit of shock and roll
Over the moon and here we go
Time to have a pop
Didn't we do well in the Eurovision Cup?

God Save The Queen
Go go go GB
Result that's almost perfect
In our jubilee
There's Anarchy in the Ukraine
We pray it all will stop
Didn't they do well in the Eurovision Cup?

Didn't they do well?
Didn't they do well?
A good game that they played for the Eurovision Cup

Apocalypse Chow
#823 / 17:05:2022

In this food apocalypse
Just know your plaice
Coz you've had your chips

Remember The Name
#824 / 18:05:2022

Jake Daniels
Superstar
We might not know your name now
But I'm sure we'll remember it
In years and years to come

Seventeen years old
And already making waves
Seventeen years old
The world at your feet
Seventeen years old
Trailblaze and brave

To be the first
The one who stands proud
And says
This is me
Deal with it
Make of it what you will
Shout what you want
As loud as you want
But I'm not going to change
Just who I am
Or what I am

Jake Daniels
May your feet do the talking now

**Conservatives Voted Against Cutting Energy Bills
By Rejecting A Windfall Tax On Oil And Gas Providers**
#825 / 19:05:2022

The evidence is clear
The evidence is there
They chose not to help
They chose not to care

They could have used their vote
Their democratic powers
They've picked the side they're on
And it isn't ours

The Chosen ... Phew!
#826 / 20:05:2022

It wasn't a cup final
Or champion's celebration
But after all we've been through
Escaping relegation

When two nil down at half time
Depression, disbelief
Then wow – what a comeback
A poem of sweet relief

"Thank you for your words of wisdom. Some have made me laugh out loud, others have made me rage with you, and one or two have made me cry." *Jane Box*

**At Least It's A Haiku –
And It Rhymes A Bit**
#827 / 21:05:2022

Woke up this morning
With no poem in my head
So wrote this instead

Moments Of Beauty
#828 / 22:05:2022
for Sarah McQuaid

Sometimes I awake to birdsong
Blackbird melodies and song-thrush harmonies

Today I awoke with echoes of beauty
As their crystal clarity replayed

Ethereally haunting
Ghosts of song and sound spirit me away

Transfixed, transformed, entranced
Pausing to savour those sounds once more

Moments of beauty
That live on and on … and on

Pure Theatre
#829 / 23:05:2022

Going to the theatre
You usually know the story
How it ends

The same show every night
Nuanced performances and thrills
But the same finale and curtain call

Not so football
In the theatres of dreams and nightmares
Where scenarios twist and turn

Always the chance of shock, surprise
Upset and genuine heartbreak
As the narrative changes constantly

The outcome uncertain
Until the very last second
And even then …

Still nuanced performances
But the star of the show may change
Top star billing not a guarantee

Sometimes it's unlikely heroes
Or the perfect understudy taking that opportunity
Changing things from nowhere

That's drama, that's theatre
Watch it unfold
Sometimes it is unbelievable

What More Evidence Is Needed?
#830 / 24:05:2022

They say that
A picture is worth a thousand words

In that case
I'll let you find your own

As I am lost for mine

Unless I write the word guilty
A thousand times

Here We Are Again ...
#831 / 25:05:2022

Just another day
And another revelation

Just another party
Another celebration

Just another gathering
Instead of isolation

The liars are still here
Still no resignation

Apparently, Everything Below Is Irrefutable Truth
And Still No-One Does The Decent Thing
#832 / 26:05:2022

Wine day Fridays, pizza and prosecco
Bottles in a suitcase, snacks and karaoke
Fire alarms and vomit, minor altercations
In out, in out – do the okey cokey *

After-hours drinking, just what were they thinking
Morning after detritus, bins overflowing
A child's broken swing, another late night binge
Nobody knowing who is coming or is going

All the above and more, much, much more
Disrespecting security and cleaners
What's going on behind that black door?
Just imagine if all that had been us?

Four o'clock Fridays – that's' when it started
But there were no parties and nobody partied
You say sorry – and that you are humbled
Not at all – just that you've been rumbled

This may not actually be 100% true but I wasn't going to waste a good rhyme.

Move On
#833 / 27:05:2022

Move on, they all say
Now it's time to move on
And do the important things

Sorry, it was time to do the important things
While you were distracted
But you didn't

So, it is indeed time to move on
For you, for all of you
Now

Play To The Whistle
#834 / 28:05:2022

Playing football
The captain handled the ball
Deliberately in the area

"Penalty!" the opposition shouted
"Definite penalty!
Obvious, everyone can see it"

Luckily, before the whistle was blown
The captain had a chat to the referee
And was able to change the rules

So that now
Not every deliberate handball
Is an automatic penalty

Play on everybody
Just play to the whistle
Apparently, own goals are not allowed either

Looking For An Ounce
Of Common Sense
#835 / 29:05:2022

Priorities, priorities
With all things ministerial
Hark back to the good old days
Bring back the imperial

It's All In A Name
#836 / 30:05:2022
for Lester Piggott

Lester Piggott
Another of those names
I seem to have known
All my life

Forever synonymous
With his chosen sport
Not my sport of choice
But everyone knew that name

Anyone on a horse
And it was always
"Who do you think you are?
Lester Piggott?"

My brother and I
Once thought of suitable racehorse names
During a Grand National afternoon
On Grandstand

Don't know why
But we came up with The Edgerton
Only one jockey in mind
Lester Piggott

Dad said that he wished
He would open his mouth
When he talked
But it was his record that spoke volumes

Lester Piggott
Legend
Unforgettable name
Ride In Peace

Oh, Go On Then ...
#837 / 31:05:2022

Being the wishy washy woolly liberal that I am
I can only say that
While I am not a royalist
Neither am anti-royalist as such

Apart from the obvious ones
Obviously

Ideologically, fiscally
I may have reservations
About the monarchy
But strangely, not so The Queen

And while I may not celebrate wildly
For some, there is much to celebrate
And rightly so

As a grizzled, cynical adult
The jubilee does not do much for me
It didn't in seventy-seven either
Even though I was no teenage Sex Pistol

But whether we like it or not
This is historical
And history is marked
By all of this and more

Last week, in a favourite school
Sat among the red, white and blue
Singing the 'God Save The Queen'
Before a whole school picnic

Plastic flags and Poundland bunting
And the National Anthem played on
Thirty year five xylophones
Almost in time, entirely at the right time

And if nothing else, a nation of children
Have learnt to spell "Platinum" and "Jubilee"
And done colouring-in
Instead of fronted adverbials

One Thing I Don't Understand
#838 / 01:06:2022

You talk about your freedom
You talk about your rights
The right for self-defence
The right to shoot on sight
But what is right is surely wrong
When all is said and done
One thing I don't understand
America and guns

This love affair with weaponry
High performance automatics
The equation is straightforward
Simple mathematics
Guns will always equal shootings
Not so – if there's none
One thing I don't understand
America and guns

If no-one had a gun
No-one would have a bullet
No-one would have a trigger
And no-one could pull it
No-one then would need to die
Nobody – no-one
One thing I don't understand
America and guns

The right to buy something that kills
Is not a right at all
The fact that it's available
In superstores and shopping malls
Guns should be for warfare
Not schoolyards in the sun
One thing I don't understand
America and guns

In a civilised society
Just incomprehensible
That guns are so accessible
Is just so indefensible

Justify it all you want
But the simple fact – it's wrong
One thing I don't understand
America and guns
One thing I can't comprehend
Surely this has got to end
Or history repeats again
America and guns

The Choice Is Yours
#839 / 02:06:2022

So, the Jubilee is not your cup of tea
Fine

Or

The Jubilee is right up your street party
Equally fine

Each to their own
That's fine

But
Don't tell me I'm not patriotic
If I don't join in

And
Don't label me a flag loving idiot
If I do

Democracy is choice
Whether you choose to celebrate
Or choose to ignore

Both valid and respected
Democracy is the right to choose
And not to be judged for that choice

All Through The Years
#840 / 03:06:2022
Lyrics for an unsung song.

All through the years
Beacon of light
The jewel within our crown
Precious and rare
All that is right
The jewel within our crown
Humility – nobility
Perfect, the balance found
Ever glorious
The jewel within our crown

All through the years
Gracious and great
The jewel within our crown
Trusted and true
Steadfast and straight
The jewel within our crown
Humility – nobility
Perfect, the balance found
Ever glorious
The jewel within our crown

Unchanging, unfailing – your legacy will remain
Delighting, uniting– the nation throughout your reign
And long may you always prosper – now and ever more
May God bless and keep you safe as we all thank you for
Your jubilee

All through the years
Forever the same
The jewel within our crown
More than a Queen
More than a name
The jewel within our crown
Humility – nobility
Perfect, the balance found
Ever glorious
The jewel within our crown

Unchanging, unfailing – your legacy will remain
Delighting, uniting– the nation throughout your reign
And long may you always prosper – now and ever more
May God bless and keep you safe as we all thank you for
Your jubilee

We stand and salute you – our noble gracious Queen
Let no-one refute you – our noble gracious Queen
We join with this anthem and long may it loudly resound
Ever glorious
The jewel within our crown

Unchanging, unfailing – your legacy will remain
Delighting, uniting– the nation throughout your reign
And long may you always prosper – now and ever more
May God bless and keep you safe as we all thank you for
Your jubilee

Your loyalty
Your royalty
Your majesty

Flying The Flag
#841 / 04:06:2022

A nation comes together
To do what it must do
Jubilee and unity
The red, the white the blue

Flags and bunting waving
The white, the blue, the red
Let a nation come together
For other things instead

It's got to be much more than
The blue, the red, the white
It's time to come together
And put this nation right

This Will Not Be That Day ...
#842 / 05:06:2022

When I do not write a poem
Time may be tight
I have still lots to do
And I should be on my way
But today will not be that day
When I do not write a poem

It may not be one of my best
It may not be memorable
It may not get shared, liked
Or commented on as others
But today will not be that day
When I do not write a poem

There are other ideas lurking
Things I really want to write about
But want to give them more time
Give them more energy and thought
But today is not the day
When I write that poem

Today is the day
That I write this poem
The poem that will do for now
This poem

Royal Tea And Sandwiches
#843 / 06:06:2022

Palaces and pageantry, circumstantial pomp
Thousands there enjoying a really royal romp
Flags and fun and Paddington – with ma'am and marmalade
And the rain in it didn't rain on your reign and your parade

If That's A Vote Of Confidence ...
#844 / 07:06:2022

When one hundred and
Forty-eight do not want you
That is not support

Glasses, Clouds And Linings
#845 / 08:06:2022

Well, I bet you feel more confident now
After that vote of confidence

Crunch the numbers
And it seems that you won

Crunch them a bit more
And it doesn't look so rosy, does it?

Not so much a decisive victory / loss
As a hollow divisive victory / loss

Depends on which way you look at it
Glass empty or glass half full

In your case, probably half full
But no doubt soon to be emptied – cheers

So ... what of the future?
You wouldn't really know, would you?

You've only ever been interested
In the here and now

Your very own here
And your very own now

At the moment you are here
But now you won't be for much longer

Every cloud and all that
And goodness knows we've had plenty of clouds

Friends
#846 / 09:06:2022

If you laugh
I'll laugh too

If you cry
I'll cry with you

If you're sad
I'll hold your hand

I will try
To understand

I will listen
If you talk

I will follow
If you walk

If you dance
Let's dance together

We can be
Friends forever

These Fuel-ish Things
#847 / 10:06:2022

At the garage
Pump in hand
Watching numbers rise
Higher and higher

In my car
Ignition on
Watching the gauge
Not reciprocating

Back To The Future
#848 / 11:06:2022

Spent most of the day
Horizontal

Not self-induced debauchery
Just a bad back

Wish I could say
That it had been something dramatic

Like a bicycle kick-winning goal
Breakdancing or abseiling

But it wasn't
It was getting out of the bath

Probably reaching for a towel
And now I'm moving in slow motion

For a while I've been making involuntary noises
Every time I put my socks on

Moreso now, when every movement
Sounds like constipation relief

Perhaps it is my body's way
Of telling me what the future has in store

Something to look forward to
Once my back eases

Adding Insult To Injury
#849 / 12:06:2022

Not only was I hobbling
Like a pensioner, due to a troublesome back
But at The Beatles Museum
I got the over sixties concession

Shush
#850 / 13:06:2022

I'm still here you know
You may be distracted
By European wars
Rising prices, poverty
Royal occasions
And lying politicians
But I'm still here
Quietly causing chaos
Hiding in plain sight
And ruining lives

Out Of Your Sight And Out Of Your Minds
#851 / 14:06:2022

Spin it any way you wish
Unless you are Rwandan

Not the place to be for a refugee
Totally abandoned

A Bairstow
#852 / 15:06:2022
A bit like a haiku, but a structure of 6, 4 ,6, 4, 6, 6 in honour of Jonny Bairstow.

More than brute force power
Timing and art
A masterpiece at work
Transcending sport
Knocked it out of the park
No boundary too big

Apparently
#853 / 16:06:2022

Apparently
There's been a high-profile resignation
The ethics adviser
For the Prime Minister

Yes ... me too
Who knew?

Is he resigning because
He's not doing his job properly?
(The ethics adviser, that is)

Or
Because he's not doing his job properly
(The Prime Minister)?

Maybe both

Either way
Ethics seems a long way down
In the list of current priorities

Everything Here Is True
#854 / 17:06:2022

The wombat is a funny creature, the wombat is unique
No other creature has this feature, or the same physique
Guaranteed to blow your mind
What they can do with their behind
You'll be shocked at what you find
When they turn each cheek

If you watch a wombat's rear you know what it will do
You won't believe what does appear – it's strange but it is true
Original, superior
Out from its interior
Through their strange posterior
It does a cubic poo

It will baffle your little brain, total disbelief
Just how much it can produce – when it seeks relief
It's the only species
With corners on its faeces
Loads of little pieces
From way down underneath

You might think it crazy, you might think it daft
You might think it's bonkers and it's just a laugh
The wombat has its superpowers
Stacking blocks for hours and hours
Building them up into towers
The wombat plays Jenga and Minecraft

It may be cute and cuddly, a friendly furry bear
It's weird, wild and wonderful what's going on in there
A squash, a squeeze, a nudge
A little bottom budge
Out pops chocolate fudge
And a brownie square

Eighty Days Of Years
#855 / 18:06:2022
for Paul McCartney

Sir Paul, Macca
Happy birthday
You seem to have been with me
All my life

An ever-present soundtrack
Probably, never a time
When I wasn't aware of you
And your music

Even at primary school
When my primary interest
Was football – and football
You were there in the background

We all knew 'Yellow Submarine'
And even made up our own daft words
One school dinnertime …
"We all live in a yellow salad cream"

And we all, and I mean all
Wanted to be a moptop in a school play
Singing "Yeah yeah yeah!"
Not knowing anything about "she" and "love"

Plus, I coveted the plastic ukulele
Uncle Bill had in his shop
That never became a present
For birthday or Christmas

But – you were not my band
That was Slade and nineteen seventy-three
Although you have always been there
Like osmosis, we all just knew the songs

And what songs!
Songs of quality and distinction
Aging like fine wines
Just getting better and better

Ahead of your time
We still haven't caught up
Still finding new things to hear
New magic, new relevance

Three-minute symphonies
Grand piano masterpieces
Timeless melodies
Unassuming genius

So, thank you Sir Paul
Happy birthday Macca
We raise a glass and raise our thumbs
Fab

Every Day
#856 / 19:06:2022

Doesn't have to be Father's Day
To think about dad
Think about him most days
To be honest

The younger I was
The more I didn't want to be like him
The older I get
The more I'd like to be him

Even at near pensionable age
I still feel like a child
When I think about him
Every day is Father's Day

There's More Than One Queue On The M62
#857 / 20:06:2022

Motorway traffic, grinds to a halt
Don't know the cause, don't know the fault
Stationery. Still. No way through
But there's more than one queue on the M62

Engines off on the carriageway
All the children – out to play
Hard-shoulder grass, a makeshift loo
But there's more than one queue on the M62

Nowhere to go in the evening sun
Here for hours, no chance of fun
But what's that? Give us a clue …
There's more than one queue on the M62

Mister Whippy on the inside lane
Opens up for trade again
A man's gotta do what a man's gotta do
When there's more than one queue on the M62

Hard shoulder walking, an orderly line
For raspberry sauce and a ninety-nine
Unexpected – strange, but true
There's more than one queue on the M62

The word gets round – a steady stream
Everybody wants ice cream
As the sun sets in the blue
There's more than one queue on the M62
For the ice cream man with the ice cream van
The ice cream queue on the M62

All Grown Up But Still Children
#858 / 21:06:2022

For the first time in our adult lives
Actually
For the first time in our lives
We are out
Together

Without parents or partners
Just the four of us
Two brothers, two sisters
And it is good, really good

In a pub garden in the sunshine
It may be the Methodists in us
Or the fact we are all driving
With two cokes and two elderflower and lemonades

We talk of those things
That hold us all together
We may be very different
But so much is the same

So much is still in place
More than we had forgotten
Those references and jokes
That only a family could know and understand

And we laugh
Really laugh
And when it is time to leave
We all have the same questions

Why haven't we done this before?
Why did we leave it so long?
When can we do it again?
Soon

Blackpool Tower And Fish And Chips
#859 / 22:06:2022

Wherever I drive
The world's biggest bottle of
Vinegar is there

Worlds Apart
#860 / 23:06:2022

Those who talk of strikes
And say it's unforgivable
Have never faced restrictions
Where wages are unliveable

As Plain As The Ever-Lengthening Nose On Your Face
#861 / 24:06:2022

Two by-election swings
Two by-elections lost
The public have their say
And you must count the cost

Now your party chairman
Has decided to resign
Can't you see the warning signs
And read between the lines?

Better Than This
#862 / 25:06:2022

Even your ex-chairman
Knows something is amiss
When he says the people
Deserve better than this

The pressure mounts once more
And yet you still resist
Even though we all deserve
Better than this

Not a minor blip
That you can just dismiss
The fact remains we all deserve
Much better than this

But blinkered, blind and blustering
Your arrogance persists
While we all deserve
Much better than this

Your velvet platitudes
In an iron fist
Shows that you don't want
Better than this

The point is made again
The point you choose to miss
You don't believe we deserve
Better than this

We just cannot accept
It is just what it is
It's time we all demanded
Better than this

Matters Of Life And Death
#863 / 26:06:2022

Americans are
So pro-life they prove it with
Their right to bear arms

Time Standing Still
#864 / 27:06:2022

Took my watch off at mum's to do the washing up
Didn't put it back on when I left

So here I am, over a hundred miles away
Not knowing the exact time but knowing that

Time has stopped at mum's
In so many ways

Not War
#865 / 28:06:2022

Missiles at a shopping centre
Not a special military operation
Not war
Missiles at a shopping centre
Not an ongoing battle for strategic positions
Not war
Shoppers are not soldiers
Not taking arms against you
Not war
Shoppers buying bread and milk
Clothes and gifts, coffee and cake
Not war
Missiles at a shopping centre
re murderous malevolent evil
Not war

What Is Mine Is Yours
#866 / 29:06:2022
A poetical response to 'I Wanna Be Yours' by John Cooper Clarke.

The final Rolo in the packet
And my favourite leather jacket
Plus – the shirt from off my back – it
Don't matter much you see
Don't care if you disagree
Cos this is how it's gonna be
What is mine is yours

My forty-fives and my LPs
From The Goodies to The Three Degrees
The last toothpaste that you can squeeze
The optimum place to watch TV
The optimum place on our settee
You're the place I wanna be
Cos what is mine is yours

The bubbled bath before I get in
The ticket from the gig we met in
All those folks I keep upsettin'
The old guitar I've never played
A photo signed by three of Slade
All the bills I haven't paid
What is mine is yours

My wellington boots for when you go
To the garage in the snow
The secrets that you still don't know
A black and white print by David Bailey
All the poems I'm writing daily
You can even have my ukulele
What is mine is yours

My sherbet dib-dabs one last dip
I'll gladly give you my last chip
And this cold sore on my lip
A P.G. Wodehouse first edition
'Love Me Do' in mint condition
A policy still to yield fruition
What is mine is yours

The cake I buy to treat myself
All the dust on my bookshelf
For what it's worth, my worldly wealth
What is mine is yours
My umbrella in the rain
I'll tell you time and time again
You know it's true – just what I'm sayin'
What is mine is yours

My coffee pot and teddy bear
All the oxygen in my air
You are sunny, I will share
Whether you want all this or not
All this stuff – you have got
You know what, you call the shots
What is mine is yours
All of this and so much more
Just one kiss, no applause
What is mine
What is mine
What is mine's
No longer mine
Now's the time
Now's the time
For what is mine is yours

Planning Ahead
#867 / 30:06:2022

Trying to get ahead of the game
Trying to plan ahead
Today's poem prepared
Written last night instead

Hoping there are no surprises
Lurking in the news
Nothing inspirational overnight
I really should have used

Nothing that's earth shattering
Nothing glaring missed
Nothing that I should have used
On my poetry list

But working on the punchlines
So cleverly I've mastered
If all else fails, this is still true
Putin's still a murdering bastard

**Poem Where The Last Two Lines May Have Been Uttered
By A Prominent Member In Parliament**
#868 / 01:07:2022

Whether it's rumour or whether it's truth
Whether there's evidence, whether there's proof
It's now an image I just can't remove ...

Sleaze

Good turn returner, favour bestower
Just who was the whistle blower
Can you stoop a little lower ,,,

Please

Probably The Best Ad Lib I've Never Used
#869 / 02:07:2022

Yesterday
I was guest speaker
At a lovely school event

Before I took the stage
Various housekeeping and thanks
Were offered to staff and parents

Tori was one such recipient
And duly got a rousing
Response and appreciative applause

Turning to the Head, I whispered
"Well, it's a long, long time
Since a Tory has had such a good reception"

He laughed and said
"I bet you daren't use that in your speech"
He was right

I didn't
Probably the best ad lib
I've never used

Community
#870 / 03:07:2022

There is something about a room full of people
Who have come together for the same purpose

They have chosen to be there at the same time
Gathered with the same aim in mind

A church room, but not church, yet totally church
Spirit, community, togetherness, warmth

Not bread, not wine – but pies and peas
This is our monthly communion

Before sharing the blessing of music and words
The same every time but different every time

Special every time, we leave uplifted
Looking forward to when we shall meet again

Picture Imperfect
#871 / 04:07:2022

Today
I have been asked to bring
Photo identity
Not my driving license
But a childhood snap
Any childhood snap

So
I am carrying
The ubiquitous primary school photo
You know the type
Where we all looked the same
Mother's best effort at a haircut
More based on economy than style
And certainly not fashion
Unless the fashion was
Crimping scissors bowl cut fringe

Inevitably toothless
But still smiling
As we all seemed to do back then

Fifty-odd years later
I still have hair
And am thankful for that
Nostalgia is a great thing
When you remember the good old days
And not even the memory of that
Crimping scissors bowl cut fringe
Can spoil it

Foundlings
#872 / 05:07:2022

I very nearly didn't go
Invited to the Foundlings Museum
For a photo opportunity with others
Who had grown up in care
Been fostered or adopted

The latter was me
My story, spectacularly unspectacular
No childhood trauma
Unless you count mum's haircuts
Or losing to dad at football, well … everything

Utterly loved and totally cared for
It is hard to imagine it being different
Or indeed … better

But so glad I went
Standing shoulder to shoulder
With similar others
Not every story a triumph over adversity
But simply a triumph of ordinary happiness

And here I am on a photo for a national publication
Stood between a comedian and rock star
Sharing stories, memories, common ground
And the reasons we are here today

Like I said, I very nearly didn't,
Thought it might be too long a journey
And too much trouble for such a fleeting occasion
But I did and I'm so glad I did
And would travel twice the distance
To do so again

Special
We are all special
And today has celebrated that

If Only There Was Something Of Note
To Write About Today ...
#873 / 06:07:2022

All this resigning and plotting
Shows the whole of the barrel is rotten
Lower than low
Blow after blow
Not just Pincher scraping the bottom

Still Not Gone
#874 / 07:07:2022

I am Titanic and the iceberg hasn't won
Going, going, going ... still not gone
You must strive for what is right and I have done no wrong
Going, going, going ... still not gone
Defeat is not a word I speak for one who is so strong
Going, going, going ... still not gone
A king amidst the traitors, just look what they've all done
Going, going, going ... still not gone
While treachery surrounds me, mine eyes will face the sun
Going, going, going ... still not gone
The times they may be changing but I don't sing that song
Going, going, going ... still not gone
A fat lady is singing yet still I'm clinging on
Going, going, going ... still not gone
The bells they may be tolling – let them ding and dong
Going, going, going ... still not gone
Betray me at your peril, one by one by one
Going, going, going ... still not gone
The circles, they diminish ... and then there were none
Going, going, going ... still not gone
The chapter may be finished but the ending's far too long
Going, going, going ... still not gone
The man who would be king was the jester all along
Going, going, going ... still not gone

A Poem Whereby Gareth Southgate Drops Harry Kane And Raheem Sterling, Resigns From Being England's Head Coach, But Decides He Wants To Manage Them To The World Cup Anyway
#875 / 08:07:2022

Like a smell that lingers
Strong and far too long
A farce within a farce
What a carry on

Belligerent and brash
From the bumbling bombshell blond
A farce that stars an arse
What a carry on

Constitutionally right
Yet morally so wrong
A farce of many parts
What a carry on

Fifty-nine and counting
And still he hasn't gone
A farce beyond a farce
What a carry on

A farce to end all farces
A farce is what it is
A Bojo Con Production
Carry On Taking the Piss

Two Words
#876 / 09:07:2022

Take your parties and your lies
Just go
Take your jolly clown disguise
Just go
Take your bumbling delusion
Take your clichés, fake confusion
Your corrupted constitution
Go
You've had too much of our time
And now the answer's "No"
Please Prime Minister
Just go

Take your blatant disregard
Just go
Them's the breaks, however hard
Just go
Take your non-integrity
Your lack of morality
And no common decency
Go
We're all sick and we're all tired
Of the Boris Johnson show
Please Prime Minister
Just go

Take your ego and control
Just go
Your empty, blackened, selfish soul
Just go
Take your narcissistic greed
All your cronies and your greed
Every sordid dirty deed
Go
Take your failings, every one
Every body blow
Please Prime Minister
Just go

Take your stupid unkempt hair
Just go
All the untucked shirts you wear
Just go
Take your cheese and take your wine
Your entitled party line
Overdue but now's the time
Go
Leave means leave means leave
As Brexiteers all know
Please Prime Minister
Just go

Take this fake buffoonery
Just go
The Bunter-lite cartoonery
Just go
Take your crass duplicity
Poison and toxicity
All your moral bankruptcy
Go
Goodbye and good riddance
You reap all that you sow
Please Prime Minister
Just go

Everybody's had enough
Of all your superficial stuff
Be you sacked or overthrown or simply just struck off
Two words Mister Johnson
… Just go

"Thoughtful and intelligent - pity our government isn't too!"
Jen Tyler Stevens

A Shining Example To Us All
#877 / 10:07:2022

When the latest Minister for Education
Andrea Jenkyns
(Yes, I had to look her up too
Hard to keep up these strange days)
Walked past the press into Downing Street
Her response to awkward questions
Was a simple gesture

To raise her middle finger
Yes
To raise her middle finger

An adult in a post of responsibility
An adult in a position of trust
An adult who should know better
An adult who should behave as such

And not like a petulant child
So, when pupils are faced with awkward questions
Are they too allowed a similar response
With a petulant middle finger to the teachers?

Her pathetic response?
"I'm only human"
Already she has shown
Her true colours

Already, she has shown herself
To be unsuitable
Already she has shown herself
To be untrustworthy

I am not a government minister
In a position of trust and responsibility
Just a poet but this poem
Metaphorically returns that gesture

Miss Jenkins
Please go
Now
Already we have seen enough

Choices ...
#878 / 11:07:2022

Pick a card, any
Card – there's no aces in the
Pack – only jokers

Yet another hat
Thrown into the ring – not one
Fit for queen or king

Think of a number
Any number – it does not
Matter – all are wrong

No Politics Today,
Just Squirrels That Are Grey
#879 / 12:07:2022

A hazelnut spread contraceptive
Is making grey squirrels receptive
They first masticate
And then procreate
But their nuts are no longer effective

Is There One Who Really Stands Out?
#880 / 13:07:2022

The fact there are so many
For a leadership election
Just shows the lack of leaders
And even less direction

In-fighting and back-biting
At every opportunity
Highlights all divisions
And the lack of unity

Summer Hull-iday
#881 / 14:07:2022

On a day like this
When the sky is pure azure
And brightly shines the
Mediterranean sun
Even the Humber sparkles

Newlands Avenue
Gloriously green and lush
Canopied and wide
Boulevards of hazy rays
Doesn't feel like Hull at all

It Must Be A Metaphor For Something
#882 / 15:07:2022

I'm wearing a mask
While writing today's poem
Will it go viral?

Too Hot For Poetry
#883 / 16:07:2022

This poem
Was going
To be cool
Refreshing
Like an ice
Lolly on a
Sunny day
B
U
T
J
U
S
T   m e l t e   d   a

w

a

y

No Forecast Needed, Same As It Ever Was
#884 / 17:07:2022

As temperatures are set to soar
To unprecedented and dangerous levels
In the Chequers area
What can only be described
As an extremely low front
Persists and continues to be at odds
With the rest of the country

Orange Cordial Ice Lollies
#885 / 18:07:2022

I remember the long hot summers
When tarmac melted
Ladybirds swarmed
And sweat flowed like rivers

Mum's homemade ice lollies
Orange cordial with stick
In the ice cube tray
They couldn't freeze fast enough

There being four of us
Plus the friends who were always round
Mum's emphasis was always on economy
Rather than taste

So one good suck
The taste and colour disappeared
And the orange lolly
Was just an ice lolly

But it was cool
And that was all that we needed
Until the next one
And the next one

Fairy Liquid Water Pistols
#886 / 19:07:2022

No mega blaster super splashers for us
Just Fairy Liquid water pistols

Filled to the brim at the kitchen sink
Hoping all the bubbles had gone

The strongest squeeze – the longest squirt
The highest arc applauded and cheered

Pretending the liquid was Star Trek lasers
Or the bullets from Kid Curry

And always at least one of us, side on
The bottle at waist level, showing off

The strongest squeeze, the longest wees
A jolly wheeze on days like these

Bought A Hat And Stayed Inside
#887 / 20:07:2022

Previous temperatures defied
Bought a hat and stayed inside

Curtains drawn, shade applied
Bought a hat and stayed inside

Online cooling tips all tried
Bought a hat and stayed inside

Ice cream breakfast – gratified
Bought a hat and stayed inside

Lolly sales have multiplied
Bought a hat and stayed inside

On car bonnets, eggs are fried
Bought a hat and stayed inside

Tarmac bubbles, roads subside
Bought a hat and stayed inside

Buckled tracks and no train ride
Bought a hat and stayed inside

Runways melt, planes denied
Bought a hat and stayed inside

Fires start, grass has dried
Bought a hat and stayed inside

Britain's burning, far and wide
Bought a hat and stayed inside

Houses burnt, people died
Bought a hat and stayed inside

Famous Last Words
#888 / 21:07:2022

Cometh the hour, cometh the clown
Trivial once again
Beyond a joke, no-one laughs
Graceless to the bitter end
"Mission largely accomplished"
A phrase so vague and hazy
And the best that you could leave us with ...
Hasta la vista baby

Believe your own achievements
Credit where it isn't due
You wanted to be the hero
We all know that isn't you
Your final words – sound absurd
From an action hero, maybe
But a PM – disgraced again
Hasta la vista baby

Hasta la vista baby
The words of a Terminator
A better choice of cliché
"See you later alligator"
Or "in a while crocodile"
Like the tears of regret lately
Your judgement day and all you say is
Hasta la vista baby

A soundbite that sounds like a fight
A joke to cheer the masses
Once again into the breach
Appease the clapping classes
Leave 'em with a smile and go
Hazy, shady, lazy
So it's hasta la vista
Goodbye mister
Hasta la vista
Lie persister
Hasta la vista
Truth twister

Common sense advice resister
He'll grope your mum and snog your sister
As welcome as a pus-filled blister
You won't be back to drive us crazy
A parting shot – that's your lot
Is that really all you've got …
Hasta la vista baby

**Different Faces,
Same Values**
#889 / 22:07:2022

There's a lot that is fishy 'bout Rishi
Little to trust about Truss

One thing they've both got in common
Neither is one of us

Now It's Time To Raise Your Game
#890 / 23:07:2022

Hey Keir, now the time is near
Things can't really stay the same
It's time to stand and make a change
It's time to really raise your game

Hey Keir, if you've ears to hear
There's only so much you can blame
On all the rubbish gone before
It's time to really raise your game

Hey Keir, please allay the fear
You're Tory grey in all but name
Just show us what you're standing for
It's time to really raise your game

Hey Keir, though it may appear
The status quo, it will remain
Just tell us what you'd really do
It's time to really raise your game

Hey Keir, please don't disappear
Now you're firmly in the frame
Just put us in your picture
It's time to really raise your game

Hey Keir, now it's time to steer
A clear direction and proclaim
Policies and promises
It's time to really raise your game

Hey Keir, if you can't win from here
With them in tatters, lost and lame
Then there is no future hope
It's time to really raise your game

Hey Keir, be more buccaneer
May truth and justice be your aim
Keir, be a pioneer
Be king of that wild frontier
Go and get your house in gear
But most of all, be sincere
And clear when you up your game

I Once Was Christopher Goldsmith
#891 / 24:07:2022

In August nineteen sixty-one
For a very short time
I once was Christopher Goldsmith

Before I was Paul
Before I was northern
I was an Essex boy
I once was Christopher Goldsmith

More Essex baby
As twists of time, procedure, fate and faith
Conspired to work their magic
And whisk me into the arms of Lancashire

Mine was chance and circumstance
Theirs was choice and love
Together we started to make sense of a world
Not complete for either of us

I had a need – but did not know it then
They had a need – I did not know it then

Christopher Goldsmith
Lived for a month, two at the most
Then quietly died, slipped away
Almost never existing

Meanwhile, Paul took his place
And grew
Not a cuckoo
But somewhere that did not start as home
Became home
And what was once home
Never was

And so, over half a century later
Nearer to the end of the journey
Than the beginning
Those questions arise
And may remain unanswered
But arise anyway

Christopher died
That I might have life
And have it more abundantly

Beyond The Fringe
#892 / 25:07:2022

Yesterday
My picture made the front page
The Observer, New Review

Not just mine
But fifteen others
A selection from fifty-nine

All of us, as children
Brought up in care, fostered
Or – in my case – adopted

Asked for a childhood photo
I quickly found the first
I could put my hand to

Ubiquitous sixties school snap
Bad fringe and missing teeth
Not knowing where it might end up

Had I known that it might be
Part of a front page spread
I might have given it more thought

Having said that
I doubt if could have found
A picture that was any better

I might have had
The full complement of teeth
But the fringe was ever thus

Thanks mum!
No – genuinely, thanks mum
For everything

Pride
#893 / 26:07:2022

The lionesses
Prepare to roar once more
Greatness is waiting

National Pride – Lionesses
#894 / 27:07:2022

Football played the way it should
Quality that's understood
More than that – more than good
Hail the victories and successes
National pride – Lionesses

Heart and soul and drive and fight
The skill and will to get it right
Gets the job done on the night
A team that works – and impresses
National pride – Lionesses

No-one feigning injury
Or shouting at the referee
Honesty and energy
No ego drama queen excesses
National pride – Lionesses

When the Lionesses score
Hear the crowd join in the roar
Everybody wanting more
Back heel tricks and flicks expresses
National pride – Lionesses

Almost through those Wembley gates
For our nation saving greats
Legendary status waits
No-one bullies, no-one messes
With …
Our national pride of Lionesses

Refreshing Change
#895 / 28:07:2022

Watching the Euros and ...

No play acting
No diving
No cheating
No dissent
No mouthing of obscenities
No sweary singing from the stands
No unwanted hand gestures
No objects thrown onto the pitch
No lighting of flares
No sexist or racist chants
No pitch invasions

Just

Total team support
Total crowd involvement
Total family atmosphere
Total football experience

"Paul Cookson is on the ball with poetry and life in the here and now."
Michael Rosen

The Voice Of Our Childhoods
#896 / 29:07:2022
for Bernard Cribbins

Throughout my life
You always seem to have been around
Somewhere

Like a favourite daft uncle
Or latterly, a genial grandpa
But always ready to entertain

With a twinkle in your eye
A quip on the tip of your tongue
And a smile upon your lips

Holes in the ground
And cups of tea were different
And eminently quotable because of you

From The Railway Children
To Jackanory and The Wombles
You were the voice of our childhoods

Ah, the good old days
Where you carried on and carried on
Fawlty Towers, Doctor Who and beyond

Never stopped, always you
In retrospect, you are the Time Lord
Always worth watching

Always worth listening to
Comic genius, perfect timing
And all-round good bloke as well

Forever may you womble free
And if in doubt – another cup of tea
Rightly said, here's a toast
To one of those we've loved the most

Distracted
#897 / 30:07:2022

I should be writing poems about
Corporate greed
Gross profit that is really gross
Immoral business practises
And the fact that nothing is being done

But I'm still distracted by Bernard
Listening to 'Gossip Calypso' for very first
Second, third and fourth time
'Winkle Picker Blues'
And smiling

With another cup of tea
Righto

The more I listen
The more I love

Today's The Day
#898 / 31:07:2022

Today's the day that dreams are made
Today's the day the match is played
The match where we won't be afraid
Today's the day to raise the stakes
Stand side by side with all the greats
One more final step awaits

Today's the day we are that team
Today's the day to live that dream
And go to where we've never been
Today's the day we've waited for
The day the Lionesses roar
Shoot, score, so much more

Today's the day for history
Today's the day for victory
Memory and legacy
Today's the day to all abide
Standing side by side by side
And celebrate our National Pride

Never Been Prouder
#899 / 01:08:2022

Sport defines moments
Even more so when victory is the emotion
This is that time we will all remember
The day we will never forget
Indelible and permanent
The occasion when you brought it home

History and legacy
Forever bound together
I've never shouted louder
Never been prouder

A nation brought together
No divisions today
All those other nearly times
All those other almost days
So near and yet so far matches
But today will never fade away
When you brought it all home

History and legacy
Forever bound together
I've never shouted louder
Never been prouder

Thank you for the highs
Thank you for the magic
The tension and the heart rate
The goosebumps and the tears
The glitter and the smiles
The elation and the celebration
When you made football home

History and legacy
Forever bound together
I've never shouted louder
Never been prouder

We have been inspired
Moved beyond expectation
Seen football through new eyes
Both on and off the pitch
You have taught us lessons
And we love it and want more
Let this moment be the catalyst
For a new beginning and a new home

History and legacy
Forever bound together
I've never shouted louder
Never been prouder

This is football
This is how it should be

Sithee
#900 / 02:08:2022

Apparently
Yesterday was Yorkshire Day
So, being down to earth and straightforward
I joined in

Drank Yorkshire tea
Read t'Yorkshire Post
Was miserable all day long
And spent nowt

Inordinately proud
I spoke as I found
And called a spade a spade
(Not being sure what the alternative is)

Declared myself a republic
At the expense of all other republics
And got involved in a little casual stereotyping
Sithee

Inconceivable
#901 / 03:08:2022

I can't conceive of a million
Let alone seven billion

Neither can I conceive of greed
In such time of human need

Out Of The Question
#902 / 04:08:2022

You shout and spout it loud and proud
How you can solve our national problem

When you're part of the party that caused them
Just how can we trust you to solve 'em?

Tanka Very Much ...
#903 / 05:08:2022

Today is the day
My new book was not published
And my new Fringe show
Did not start its sold out run
Still – it's a good drying day

Rishi The Lying Heart
#904 / 06:08:2022

Redistribute resources
As there has been a glitch
So I'll take back from the poor
And give more to the rich

Like Robin Hood – but in reverse
Rishi and his merry band
That's merry band of bandits
Pillaging this land

Time To Shine
#905 / 07:08:2022
for Jim Lea and Don Powell, Wolverhampton Museum

Once upon a time ago ... behind glitter boots and mirrors
Two men in the shadows – not everyone remembers
The other two, the quiet ones – half the equal crucial four
But still you caused the riot ones ... rock and roll and so much more

    Now it is your time to shine
    To claim the spotlight truly yours
    Now, the time to recognise
    Just who you are – to stop and pause

Forever that connection – to the band that shaped our lives
No longer now confined – to those times we memorise
The backbone and the heart and soul – down to earth, humbly human
The backbeat for the rock and roll ... gentlemen, unassuming

    Now it is your time to shine
    To claim the spotlight truly yours
    Now, the time to recognise
    Just who you are – to stop and pause
    Now the time to redefine
    Your contributions, your rewards

Where the magic all begins – and everybody has their place
Bass and drums and violins – the metronome that keeps the pace
The perfect pair, the rhythm twins – the rumble of the fluid bass
Emerging from the shadowed wings – happy now, centre stage

    Now it is your time to shine
    To claim the spotlight truly yours
    Now, the time to recognise
    Just who you are – to stop and pause
    Now the time to redefine
    Your contributions, your rewards
    Now it is your time to shine
    To receive your true applause

Reluctant stars perhaps
But all the stars shine bright these days

It just depends on where you look
Just depends on where you gaze

Now it is your time to shine
To claim the spotlight truly yours
Now, the time to recognise
Just who you are – to stop and pause
Now the time to redefine
Your contributions, your rewards
Now it is your time to shine
To receive your true applause
To receive your true applause
To receive … your true … applause

Half Of Slade And My Best Mate, Les
#906 / 08:08:2022

If someone had said this was possible
In nineteen seventy-three
I'd have said
Dream on, no way

If someone had predicted this
Amongst the glam rock Top of the Pops madness
I'd have said
It was just that – madness

If someone had told me we'd be friends
And share a stage
I'd have said
Never in a month of Sundays

Yet, there we were
Half of Slade and my best mate
Jimmy, Don, Les and me
How does it feel?

Just right

Yes, There Was So Much More To You Than This ... But ...
#907 / 09:08:2022
for Olivia Newton-John

That moment comes to mind right now

I don't even have to mention the film
We all know
We just know

Everyone – and I mean everyone
Knew about you
Everyone talked about you

That song, that smile
Those moves and yes ...
Those trousers

Iconic, eternal
And in that moment
You were the one that we wanted

Or the one we wanted to be
It was summer – it was love – sensational

Yes indeed

You were so much more
The hits carried on
Evergreen, your star never waned

Loved by all
Still loved by all
Yes indeed

Olivia Newton ... gone

The Final Verse Is Not A Haiku
But You'll Have To Count To Find Out Why
#908 / 10:08:2022

Born in sixty-one
Just where has that time all gone
Now I'm sixty-one?

Time travels faster
Running further away while
I just get slower

I've had more birthdays
Than I'll have again so best
Make the most of them

Not cards or gifts but
Family and friends

More Than Just Pictures
#909 / 11:08:2022
for Raymond Briggs

Fungus was always my favourite
Especially the plop up version
And if you had only published one book
It would have been enough to make you iconic

But of course, there was so much more
Heart, humanity and humour
Fantasy maybe but rooted in reality
All from your pen

Instantly recognisable
It could only have been you
Such a body of work
Such a legacy

Raymond Briggs
Thank you

Reality. Check. Mate ...
#910 / 12:08:2022

The problem with getting
A new collection of poems
By Roger McGough
Is realising
You still have so much to learn

I mean
I've started this poem
So I suppose I'd better finish it

But I'm no mastermind
Unlike Roger

Not The Poem I Had In Mind
#911 / 13:08:2022

This is not the poem I had in mind
Not the poem I was going to write today

That one had elements of love and tolerance
Peace, goodwill and acceptance

Instead, I am writing about knives and hate
And a writer attacked at a public event

So, this is not the poem I had in mind
But its final words will be to send out love

I Wish I Could Say It Was The Result Of ...
#912 / 14:08:2022

A last-minute goal-scoring bicycle kick
A unicycle circus trick

Match point serve, rapid ace
That put my back out of place

A triple somersault, so dramatic
Or something likewise acrobatic

Abseiling down the Blackpool Tower
Butterfly swimming for seventeen hours

A breakdance dance or a moonwalk groove
My table tennis signature move

The bounciest bounce on the trampoline
The best high dive you've ever seen

Rope swing Tarzan, climbing trees
Daring-do on the flying trapeze

Surfing waves on the highest seas
The whoosh and rush of black run skis

Alas – alack – none of these ...

At my age ... you're having a laugh
I tweaked it getting out of the bath

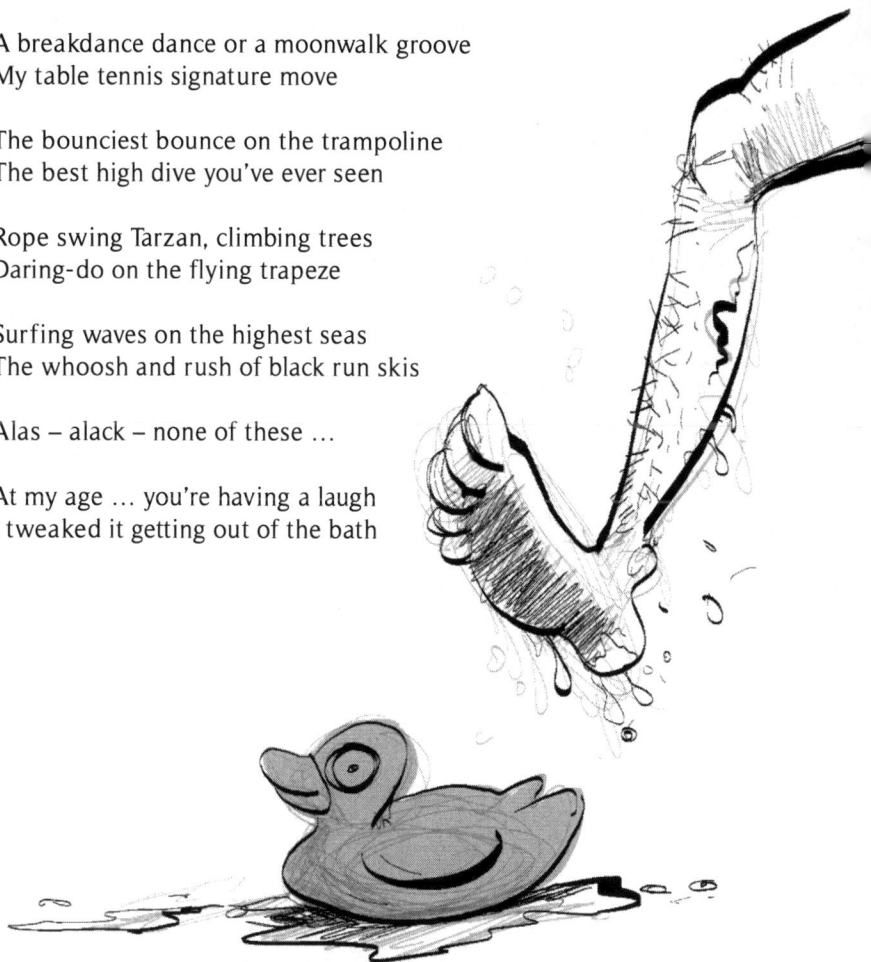

Nake
#913 / 15:08:2022

It's been here all day
The Nake
Yesterday as well
And the day before that
Probably tomorrow too
Looks like it's here to stay
Causing mischief and trouble
Niggling persistently
Slowing me down with its constant attack
Cause I've got a Nake, a Nake in my back

Walking Stick
#914 / 16:08:2022

We never threw it away
The one we bought dad for his fiftieth
We thought it ancient then
Now fifty seems ancient history for all of us
He never used it that much
But enough to be his
The carved dog's head handle
Wood worn from those hands
Probably striding across the fields
Or poking about in nettles
And now, I have a reason
To use it as it should be used for a day or so
Shame it didn't have a
Norse's 'ed 'andle
Then my northern-ness
Would be complete

Meanwhile, Back To Politics
And Two Dictionary Definitions
#915 / 17:08:2022

A Sunak – money eating reptile
Or a smiling liar bluffing it

A Truss – surgical support for bollocks
What you do to a chicken before stuffing it

Numerically Dyslexic
#~~942~~ #916 / 18:08:2022

I apologise
I appear to have misled you, numerically
I have indeed written a poem every day, but the numbers …

Somewhere along the line, or lines
There has been a typo, at least one
As I seemed to jump twenty-six poems ahead

Also, a few days when I wrote two poems
To add further confusion
Anyway, I seem to have worked this out now

Back on track and not wanting to get it wrong
As I head towards poem one thousand
That would be embarrassing

So, this is poem nine one six not nine forty-two
Sorry about that – unless the twenty-six poems have been lost
Shame – I bet they were among my best

"Get Back To Work – You Fat Ponce!"
#917 / 19:08:2022

On holiday again from Number Ten
Our workshy vacant – PM
One holidaymaker's swift response
"Get back to work – you fat ponce!"

One lone loud voice and circumstance
We'd have said the same, given half a chance
Clear as a bell – just once
"Get back to work – you fat ponce!"

Straight to the point – seven small words
A mystery man – unseen but heard
A shout out shoot out at the bleached blond bonce
"Get back to work – you fat ponce!"

So now it's relaxation and downtime
Like Number Ten with Greek sunshine
Usual casual nonchalance
"Get back to work – you fat ponce!"

We understand that he is lazy
But back to work? You must be crazy!
No more damage please from this dunce
"Get back to work – you fat ponce!"?

"Get back to work – you fat ponce!"?
Especially when it's Boris Johns-
On – the one that no-one wants
Stay with orange juice and croissants
'Cause you've never worked – you fat …

"Oh I Do Like To Wee Beside The Seaside …"
#918 / 20:08:2022

With this current government
It seems entirely fitting
Lots of public excrement
Sea and sand with shit in

Don't Put The NHS On A Pedestal
#919 / 21:08:2022

So says a potential Prime Minister
And in doing so, proves something
Many of us already suspected

Truss cannot be trusted
The Tories cannot be trusted
Simple

The NHS should be
On the highest pedestal possible
The jewel within our crown

A prized asset
Valued, funded
And freely available to all

Some things are more than economics
Cost effective balance sheets
The NHS is one such thing

Ask most people
And they will want it central
Important to our society

So, as far as pedestals go
What could go on a higher pedestal
Than the commitment to care

Which is why
When a potential Prime Minister
Says these words

We all know instinctively
That they are wrong
And have been all along

"Beautiful, caring, honest words. More support in this lovely
meaningful poem than all the media together." *John Leonard*

How Can Anyone Involved
Look At Themselves In The Mirror
And Truly Say They Have Done The Right Thing?
#920 / 22:08:2022

Sewage galore
Rank and raw
Allowed to pour
On beach or shore

And what's more
They voted for
Passed the law
Chose to ignore

So ... This Is Okay? Right?
#921 / 23:08:2022

Oh
To be a CEO
Pay rise of thirty-nine per cent

But

Don't be a nurse
Or even worse
Don't strike to show your discontent

Sometimes Poetry In Progress
Is Just Emotional Journalism
Until At Least The Second Draft
#922 / 24:08:2022

This is one such day
When emotional response is instant

Horror, shock and sorrow
Are quickly followed by anger and justice

Anyone who is a parent
Even we can't fully comprehend

Anyone who has a heart
It can only be breaking right now

When a nine-year-old girl
Is shot dead in her own home

When a family is torn apart
It is not really a day for poetry

"If journalism is the first draft of history, then here is the second:
life shaped, structured, described, annotated."
Ian McMillan

The Noises That I Make When I'm Putting On My Socks
#923 / 25:08:2022

The sound of my aging is causing much discussion
My family, they mention my body's new percussion
An involuntary groan as I rise from the chair
The puffing and the panting halfway up the stair
My left knee – as first it clicks then pops
And those noises that I make when I'm putting on my socks

Is it something genetic or something more ancestral
Or just advancing years make my body more orchestral
The bagpipe like wheeze as I rise every morning
The trombones and the trumpets that blow without due warning
This flatulent fanfare that never ever stops
And the noises that I make when I'm putting on my socks

Internal organs – they have a life that's all their own
A stomach that can rumble, then grumble, gurgle, groan
Rubbing my tired eyes my eyeballs seem to squeak
A hip that just grates and shoulders that just creak
Fingers in both ears lead to audible plop-plops
And the noises that I make when I'm putting on my socks

The *ooh* and *eeh* and *aah* – if I move too quickly
The stamp when I have cramp that makes it look like Strictly
The voltage and the shock of unexpected sneezes
And as you get older their volume just increases
Displeasing wheezing and lots of noisy shocks
These sounds I seem to make
As everything just aches
And the time it takes – just putting on my socks

"I'm smiling the broadest smile reading this one." *Gareth Higgins*

At Home In A Festival Field
#924 / 26:08:2022

At home in a festival field
Here where my heart is
Waited so long for Greenbelt
And where the art is

**I Haven't Seen The News And May Have
Missed Something Important ... But ...**
#925 / 27:08:2022

What is important
Is that we are here
Again
At last

Good to be back isn't it?
No. Wrong
Not good to be back
Great

In a field with friends
Old and new
In a field with family
Deep and trusted

Learning, living
Laughing, loving
Sharing, encouraging
Communing, connecting

Together
We are together
And for these few days
That is the most important thing

Thank You
#926 / 28:08:2022

For being there
All of you who came along

All of you who joined this poetical liturgy
This connection, this literary sacrament

I could not have done this without you
Well, I could but it wouldn't be the same

Thank you so much
We are all in this together

Again
Peace be with us all

Brian Eno And Richard Dawkins
#927 / 29:08:2022

I saw two atheists
At a Christian festival
One I believed in
One I didn't

Intellect and science
May well have their place
But I'll always have more faith
In humility and grace

Greenbelt Haikus
#928 / 30:08:2022

Ooh it's fizzy wine
Not the blessing I'd hoped for
Not the worst either

What you see depends
On where you look and finding
On how you search

Dab dab dab no splish
Splash splosh – the Monday morning
Wet wipe body wash

Grace is the man with
The van and suction tubes who
Empties Greenbelt loos

A sound I'm looking
Forward to … the sound of a
Real flushing toilet

I did not believe
In his existence till I
Saw Richard Dawkins

Nothing else like it
Searching and imperfect
Where else would we go?

The Farewell Tour
#929 / 31:08:2022

Before the sun goes down on you
You want a farewell tour
A captain who wasn't fantastic
Who could have done so much more

You may still be standing
And carry on undeterred
But you won't be saying sorry
Cos that's the hardest word

Instead you want to celebrate
All that you have done
Like a candle in the wind
It shouldn't take that long

What you need's a rocket, man
We'd all watch that explode
Eton Johns-on final tour …
Goodbye Yellow Thick Toad

"Better than Bernie's lyrics." *Andrew Wells*

The Roaring Silence
#930 / 01:09:2022

The Queen is in her counting house
Counting up her votes
Lowering the bar
And lowering our hopes
The Queen in waiting, stating
That she's going to walk the walk
But The Queen is hesitating
Not prepared to talk

Not prepared to face the music
Never mind the questions
She doesn't have the answers
Just soundbites, vague suggestions
Like a rabbit in the spotlights
Wide eyes on a stalk
The Queen is keeping counsel
Far too scared to talk

This one who would be Queen
Refusing interviews
Goodness knows just how she'll cope
If it comes to PMQs
Tweeting like a sparrow
When hunted by a hawk
She wants to rule the roost
But doesn't want to talk

She dreams of being Thatcher-like
Powerful and ruthless
She's not even Thatcher-lite
Toothless and worse than useless
Her silence is not golden
More a rusty fork
Not fit for public use
And not prepared to talk

Simple Solution
#931 / 02:09:2022

Condescension hits new lows, ignorance new highs
Reality a concept that just does not apply
The solution to this crisis and to offset the debt'll
You can save ten quid a year and buy a brand new kettle

Families facing hardship, poverty and death
You tell us you're concerned and yet in the same breath
The words of wisdom you impart are all about scrap metal
And the best advice that you can give … buy a brand new kettle

Buy a brand new kettle
To keep you in fine fettle
Everything will be just fine
Buy a brand new kettle

Future trouble bubbling much worse than it might seem
Talk about hot air, boiling points and steam
Digest those actual words – let their crassness settle
And this is what you voted for … buy a brand new kettle

Buy a brand new kettle
To keep you in fine fettle
The answer to all problems …
Buy a brand new kettle

Let Your Light Shine
#932 / 03:09:2022

In these shadowed darkened times
Just let your light shine
Through these deep, depressing days
Just let your light shine

When all around seems black and bleak
Felling helpless, lost and bleak
May your actions gently speak
Just let your light shine

Obvious
#933 / 04:09:2022

Children will starve – not just the few
Families will freeze – depressingly true
Businesses close – all thanks to you
People will die – all this you knew

Your reality different – privileged distant
Still you're indifferent – blinkered, resistant
And still you chose what not to do
Still you tried nothing new

All of the blame is on you

You Know It's First Day Back At School When ...
#934 / 05:09:2022

A blazer is far too big and your mum says
"You'll grow into it"

Shoes are far too shiny
And you're learning how to tie a tie again

A new Adidas school bag or purple duffle bag
Neither written on with football teams or bands ... yet

Sharpened pencils and biros with tops on
Plus a brand new full pencil case

Including rubber, pencil sharpener, coloured pencils
Ruler, protractor and the dangerous weapon that is the compass

Spending the whole first lesson of every subject
Writing your name and form on new exercise books

And the homework was always the same ...
"What I did on my summer holidays"

And covering all your new school books
With last year's wallpaper

"Keep it up Paul. Giving a voice to many." *Cat Obbard*

Oxymoronic Final Speech By An Oxymoron
#935 / 06:09:2022

In a speech full of dubious affirmatives
Varied and vacuous superlatives
The thing most absurd
The use of two words
Compassionate and Conservatives

**There'll Be Plenty Of Days To Use The Words Truss
And Mistrust In A Poem, But Today Is Not That Day**
#936 / 06:09:2022

Leadership election
Unnatural selection
What's more to say?
Same mess, different day

You're Going To Like This ... Not A Lot
#937 / 07:09:2022

Shuffle the deck
Change the focus
Same marked cards
Pack of Jokers

"Fabulous. So much in so few words." *Sue Hardy-Dawson*

Everyday Economic Solution
From Everyday Every-Woman Auntie Edwina
#938 / 07:09:2022

So – we've all lived in houses that are old
Grown up in a home that was sometimes very cold
So never mind the price of gas and oil
You just need a bit more tin foil

Slide it down your radiator, see
How much warmer it can be just moving your settee
Always a solution – if you care to toil
Just buy a bit more tin foil

Always good to get a tip to keep you warm and healthy
From those who do not need them 'cause they are all so wealthy
So please don't let their condescension spoil
You buying that bit extra tin foil

Handy tips for getting through the winter
Here's one I made earlier, just like on Blue Peter
Next, we're learning how to cook with soil
That – and buying more tin foil

Now, to make a generator, ever so fantastic
Coat hangers, fairy bottles and sticky back plastic
A kettle made from cardboard that's cheap and safe to boil
Oh yes – and more tin foil

What we're really needing in this crisis
Is not a rich ex-minister lecturing about prices
But action and compassion amidst all this turmoil
Not more bloody tin foil

That's Liz Truss
#939 / 08:09:2022

A supply teacher suddenly asked to be the Head
The lunchtime supervisor asked to be the cook instead
The one who was conductor now asked to drive the bus
The third team reserve goalie asked to play at Wemb-er-lee
The last one on the list to take a World Cup penalty
Compared to the last negative she's only just a plus
That's Liz Truss

The woman with a barge pole, expected now to dance
The woman with the pomp and little circumstance
Teaching advanced maths – with just an abacus
From the chorus to the lead, she now stands centre stage
The asterisked appendix note is now on the front page
The shorthand typist asked to write the syllabus
That's Liz Truss

The Sunday morning flower lady asked to preach a sermon
The nursery TA now teaching A-Level German
Like Sooty's right hand woman to Doctor Octopus
Like a waitress in a café asked to cook for royalty
The one who holds the subs board up is now the referee
The one who wants a golden crown that's really made of rust
That's Liz Truss

The hospital receptionist promoted to brain surgeon
Instead of Richard Branson we end up with a virgin
When wanting earth that's rich for growth and all you get is dust
The one who played triangle's now conducting with the baton
Titanic boiler stoker now has the captain's hat on
All of the above – feel free to discuss
That's Liz Truss

Out of her depth and sinking yet still they all believe her
Moreso that she's now PM and our new great leader
A fact that is as weird as the duckbilled platypus
The con that's in Conservative, she puts the rust in trust
Lowering the bar and leaving us non plussed
And if you think comparisons like these are all unjust
Then you're going to love Liz Truss

Dignified And True
#940 / 09:09:2022

More than mere monarch
One of the chosen few
Much more than a Queen
Dignified and true

Royalty and loyalty
In everything she'd do
The jewel in our crown
Dignified and true

A national institution
Old but ever new
There'll never be another
Dignified and true

When all around her faltered
Her light would shine on through
An example to us all
Dignified and true

The straightest of straight lines
Never once askew
A journey undeterred
Dignified and true

Always, always there
She was the national glue
That held us all together
Dignified and true

Elizabeth the Great
All credit where it's due
Constancy in change
Dignified and true

Decency personified
Dignified and true
Thank you Ma'am for everything
We love you

Reflections, Lines And Unfinished Poems
#941 / 10:09:2022

Blue skies and mourning
A rainbow over Windsor
A promise of hope

I cannot think of her
Without thinking of mum or nan
Good company for all

Now is the not the time for cheap irreverence
Snide humour or talk of revolution
And if that is all you have to offer
Then let your silence be as silent
As those whose silence is from the heart

While there may be issues with The Monarchy
There are none with this monarch

If you squint I suppose it may seem
Like a heavenly sign that would mean
Her presence is nigh
A vague shape in the sky
The cloud that looked like The Queen

All is changing
The coins in my pocket
The face on my banknotes
The stamps on my letters
Soon to be
History

They are not pilgrims
Yet make a pilgrimage

There is a sense of unbelief
With all this public grief

Small bouquet?
A fiver please
Oh to be a florist
In times like these

This is not a time for everyone
At least one channel
Should be showing comedies
Especially ones that made her laugh

She got to ninety-six
Albeit with the best diet and doctors
But still – ninety-six
Not a bad innings and all that
And while it may be sad
It's all part of the cycle
A long life, a full life
A good life

Now is not a time for revolution
But then again, when is?
So maybe now is the time
To think seriously, very seriously
So we have no need of a revolution

They may have been the words of a king
But more importantly, they were the words of a son

Sonnet
#942 / 11:09:2022

Of proclamations and ascensions heed
Traditions old, we may not comprehend
Succession of the throne and yet, God's speed
King Charles the Third accept and now ascend

This mantle, this responsibility
This heritage, the pre-ordain-ed plan
This present with its root in history
The past and yet the future in one man

A figurehead and still a mother's son
The regal and the human become one
In grief and mourning, all this must be done
The crown is but a crown to be passed on

So now with one accord and voice we sing
God save, long live our noble gracious King

I Think I May Have Been Watching Too Much
Of The Royal Coverage Because
#943 / 12:09:2022

I
Am
Now
Writing
Po

Ems

Like
Nicholas
Wit
Chell
Has
Been

Spea .... King

Slow

Ly

Reveren....tially

And
Making
It
Last
As
Long
As
Is

Possible

In Other News
#944 / 13:09:2022

Police arrest man for shouting
But not two others for assault

Holding signs of disagreement is now unlawful
But fracking is legal

Marmalade sandwiches are left for the dead
But the homeless remain homeless and hungry

A rich man escapes inheritance tax
But energy prices for the poor at an all-time high

Russia loses ground in war in Ukraine
And I can now put my left sock on without grimacing in pain

And now, the weather ...

"Absolute genius." *Julie Slater*

I Didn't Know Her And I'm Not Trying To Be Presumptuous But I'm Sure She Wouldn't Want All This ...
#945 / 14:09:2022

Of all the many things I've heard
And all the things that I have seen
Checkout beeps at Morrisons
Turned down to respect The Queen?

Well, that and Center Parcs
Exercising such strange powers
Asking paying guest to leave
For twenty-four hours

Those with greatest need
Can't access the food banks
Hunger and starvation
While a nation's giving thanks

And funerals for loved ones
Must have a different date
Not now as important
As the one who lies in state

Cancer operations
Postponed and rearranged
Not saving life because of death
The truth is more than strange

Respect and decent courtesy
Must be carefully selective
More important, common sense
And practical perspective

In Line
#946 / 15:09:2022

qqqqqqqqqqqqqqqqqqqqqqqqqqqqqqqqqqqqqqqqqqqqqqqqqqqqqqq
qqqqqqqqqqqqqqqqqqqqqqqqqqqqqqqqqqqqqqqqqqqqqqqqqqqqqqq
qqqqqqqqqqqqqqqqqqqqqqqqqqqqqqqqqqqqqqqqqqqqqqqqqqqqqqq
qqqqqqqqqqqqqqqqqqqqqqqqqqueenqqqqqqqqqqqqqqqqqqqqqqqqq
qqqqqqqqqqqqqqqqqqqqqqqqqqqqqqqqqqqqqqqqqqqqqqqqqqqqqqq
qqqqqqqqqqqqqqqqqqqqqqqqqqqqqqqqqqqqqqqqqqqqqqqqqqqqqqq
qqqqqqqqqqqqqqqqqqqqqqqqqqqqqqqqqqqqqqqqqqqqqqqqqqqqqqq

As A Billion Camera Phones Click Away
Like Angry Insects Swarming,
Everyone's An Expert Now
#947 / 16:09:2022

Speculation
Exaggeration
Every detail focused
Scrutinised
Amplified
Picked apart by locusts

As A Mark Of Respect ...
#948 / 17:09:2022

This poem is hereby a notice and due warning
That in full accordance with public mood and mourning
The importance of respect in the current climate
Monday's poem is cancelled in case I try to rhyme it
As that would be a travesty
Offensive to Her Majesty
Like the few above and rightly so, the reason
Monday's poem is hereby cancelled
Just in case of treason

Just Another Week
#949 / 18:09:2022

It's what makes the country great
You wait and wait and wait and wait
To pass a coffin, laid in state
Just another week

The stillness of a church divine
A footballer who bides his time
A fallen soldier in the line
Just another week

An inkwell that is wrongly placed
Marmalade sandwiches gone to waste
Shouting at a prince disgraced
Just another week

Leaky pens, twelve-hour queues
Tearful mourners, vox pop views
Meghan Markle's high-heeled shoes
Just another week

Living breathing history
Arrested if you disagree
Letters of redundancy
Just another week

All the latest funeral plans
Justice that the press demands
A married couple holding hands
Just another week

Thousands want to play their parts
For their Queen, the Queen of hearts
For some, it's where new friendship starts
Just another week

Fast track lines for MPs
And daytime celebrities
Who haven't time to wait or freeze
Just another week

The right and wrong way that we mourn
Who can wear a uniform
Does that curtsey fit the norm
Just another week

All the lessons we've learned from her
Pageantry, a guard of honour
Just what is an Oxford comma?
Just another week

I'm getting carried by the mourning
Ding dong the funeral bells will chime
What am I doing? Joining in the queuing
I'll never get to church on time

The moving line goes on and on
And on and on and on and on
And on and on and on and on
For another week

Mourning
#950 / 19:09:2022

i.
Today we may morn
And yet something is missing
That something is u

ii.
If you find the rave in grave
A good sense of humour'll
Find the vice in service
And put the fun in funeral

Unforgettable
#951 / 20:09:2022

Sovereignty upon this chosen day
The eyes of all the world will look our way
Absolutely flawless dignity
Throughout this breathing history
Epitome of Her Majesty

Forever, let us cherish this great scene
Unilateral love for our dear Queen
Nothing left to chance, all so planned
Every careful detail, all in hand
Regal and respectful royalty
All this pomp and perfect pageantry
Lest we all forget Her Majesty

**The Nation May Have Come Together For A Brief Moment
But Things Don't Change**
#952 / 21:09:2022

After all the pomp and ceremony
The solemn and the formal
Tax cuts for the rich
Service back to normal

"Brilliant ... again." *Mark Heybourne*

BANKERS ... bankers
#953 / 22:09:2022

Following Government guidelines
This poem has been approved
According to current policy
Bankers' caps removed

This Poem Has Nothing To Do With Current World Events
But Everything To Do With My Life
#954 / 23:09:2022

There may be questions about
Territorial integrity in Ukraine
That may well be the case
But right now, I'm thinking about mum

There may be threats of nuclear retaliation
From a Russian madman
But at the moment I'm more interested
In the X-ray results

Yes, I know it's war and more than serious
But my immediate concern is closer to home
And the fact my eighty-nine-year-old mother
Didn't break anything when she fell

I'm No Economist ... But ...
#955 / 24:09:2022

If the bigger drops are at the top
They must be thinner down the line
Trickle down slowly
One drop at a time

Like glasses in a pyramid
Awaiting high class wine
Overflowing from the top
One drop at a time

So lower down the pyramid
Things aren't quite so fine
The glasses there cannot be filled
One drop at a time

Be grateful for what comes your way
Down this long and slow incline
Not much left to trickle down
One drop at a time

An economic system
Unequal by design
It can't all trickle down
One drop at a time

One drop at a time
When the situation's chronic
Is simply not enough
With trickle economics

Trickle down? The wrong way round
This all needs to stop
We need a brand new start
When things can trickle up

It may be over simplified
To say it isn't fair
Except we've got a government
Who aren't prepared to care

Poetrickledown
#956 / 25:09:2022

To reflect current government thinking I've written this poem – without rhyme or indeed reason – in such a manner that the benefits of the words herein will eventually trickle down so that everyone can enjoy them but to be honest I'm not really sure that this particular style of writing a poem is going to work very well and the words at the end may be missed as it t

a
k
e
s

s
o

l
o
n
g

t
o

g
e
t

t
h
e
r
e

**To The Socialist Left – While I May Broadly Agree
With Much Of What You Say, The Reality Is This ...**
#957 / 26:09:2022

The middle ground is the battleground
Whether you like it or not

Most aren't really bothered about left or right
Labour or Conservative at all

Revolution is not on their agenda
Radical change is not their manifesto

They just want fair
And a common sense approach

They don't really want to rock the boat
Just that the boat will float

Sink your own boat
And we all drown faster

Principles are great
But at some point we have to meet in the middle

And it doesn't have to be a bad place to be
Just a good place to start

"Such a huge achievement. We are all so grateful to have your poems
every day. They're so varied and have kept us laughing, crying and
kept us going. Thank you so much." *Claire Bartrip*

Just To Be Clear Here …
#958 / 27:09:2022

There may be differences and doubt
But first things first
Tories out

Too many things to moan about
First things first
Tories out

In an ideal world there'd be a rout
Better to have power and clout
Than just to spout and end with nowt
And stay forever on this roundabout
First things first
Tories out

One fight at a time – we know what the war is
The future's now, not past glories
But living through their horror stories
We all know just what their score is
Never mind what's gone before is
Not what's needed here much more is
One small step and if crossing the floor is
Not for you, you know where the door is
But first things first
First things first
First things first
Don't make things worse
First things first
First things first
First things first
Get rid of the Tories

Just to be clear
Hear the shout
First things first
Tories out

A Poem With A Moral
#959 / 28:09:2022

If I tell you a secret
Will you tell me yours
As longs as it's funny
And gets me applause

I'll write it in verse
Line after line
And then, even worse
I'll write it in rhyme

Build to the punchline
Poetically sleek
Then give out the secret
You told me to keep

I promised discretion
Till I heard your story
Then stole it and shared it
And got all your glory

The moral is clear
I'm sure you all know it
Never, no never
Confide in a poet

You've Got To Get To The Hunchli …
Sorry, Pun-chline Somehow
#960 / 29:09:2022

To be honest
I've absolutely no clue whatsoever
About interest rates and budgets

So, it would seem
I have much in common
With the Chancellor of the Exchequer

Does that mean then that
I'm in Kwasi mode – oh
No!

In Radio News:
New Contestant Fails Audition For Just A Minute
#961 / 30:09:2022

Er
Hesitation
Digression
Er
Hesitation
Repetition
Er
Hesitation
Digression
Er
Hesitation
Err
Hesitation …

Err … err … her …

Progressively Worse
#962 / 01:10:2022

Go further down the barrel
And you will scrape the bottom
More than one bad apple
Progressively more rotten
Everything just turns to dirt
Like Midas in reverse
The art of the Tory party
Successive leaders, progressively worse

And just when things have got so bad
And the descent should get slower
Wrong, wrong and wrong again
They sink even lower
Is it just a special talent?
Or is it now a curse?
The art of the Tory party
Successive leaders, progressively worse

Yearning for the good old days
We all knew where we stood
So much so we even say
"That John Major – he was good"
Boring? Grey? That was the way
Nothing too adverse
But the art of the Tory party
Successive leaders, progressively worse

So bad now, it has been said
"Now Thatcher was a proper leader
Her yes was yes, no was no
Even if we didn't believe her
If nothing else, she worked damned hard
And put the country first"
Now the art of the Tory Party
Successive leaders, progressively worse

Once it was a Rolls Royce
Now it is a hearse
Driving us towards our fate
Successive leaders, progressively worse

That
#963 / 02:10:2022

We grew up
Knowing that story

Those of us who lived round there
Could never drive on that motorway
Without looking over
On that desolate bleakness
And think about that horror

Even on sunny days
It was never bright
Just a never-ending shadow
On that moor
Cast by
That

About Turn
#964 / 03:10:2022

In accordance with present policy
And government example
I'm not spending much time or thought
On today's poem
As it will no doubt
Be withdrawn
And have to be rewritten
Tomorrow
And the day after
And the day after

And the day after that

Not
#965 / 04:10:2022

Not a U-turn
A change of direction
Not a different course at all
Just a different perception

Not a backward step
Merely forward thinking
Not a change of plan
Just strategic inkling

Not a compromise
An alternative plan of action
Not a sign of indecision
More one of distraction

Not a response to public feeling
More internal frictions
Business as usual then
A mass of contradictions

The Haiku Diary
Of Kwasi Kwarteng
#966 / 05:10:2022

Went to Queen's funeral
Four days later could not do
My job properly

But in retrospect
Not sure that the funeral made
Much difference really

Just realised that
Maths is not my strong point as
I can't even seem to count

Every Day Is Poetry Day
#967 / 06:10:2022

Words come and go
That is their way
Some fade away while others stay
When every day is poetry day

Be they inspired
Or just okay
Either way, come what may
When every day is poetry day

A punchline joke
Or cheap wordplay
I'm going to write them anyway
When every day is poetry day

A rambling thought
To share and say
Or silent prayer that you might pray
When every day is poetry day

A line and rhyme
An old cliche
Pen and paper – time to play
When every day
When every day
When every day is poetry day

Black To The Future
#968 / 07:10:2022

I might love the seventies
But not that much
To go back to the days
And nights of power cuts

The Future's Not Bright ...
#969 / 08:10:2022

Don't wanna go back to my youth
With every poem I'm writin'

Candle in window
Saturday night's not right for street lighting

So Here It Is ...
#970 / 09:10:2022

Don't no weather it woz the late nite
Or the fact I've bin to the Slade fanz convention
Just carnt seem too spel properlee today
Thistle hav to doo

Altho I have got a powem about a gud mate
Hoo returned from hollyday havin spent
Too much tyme in the sun
It's called *my friend's tan*

Almost That Day
#971 / 10:10:2022

Almost that day when I didn't write a poem
A busy week and even busier weekend have caught up on me

Woke feeling rough, bunged-up and already tired
Factor in a long journey and the morning was gone

Still lots to do – not all of it stress free
Yes, today was almost that day when I didn't write a poem

Almost

Somehow, I Feel Like I'm Trespassing
#972 / 11:10:2022

Mum is eighty-nine
Nearly ninety
For eighty-nine and a bit years
She has been in her own home

But not now
She is in a home
But it is not
Home

It is what it is
She is well looked after
Fed, medical needs sorted
And most importantly, safe

Here to visit
I am staying in her house
And she is not here
Yet everything about her is around me

Everything is where it always has been
For now
Things will change
But not this minute

As the clock ticks in the background
It strikes me thus
Mum will never put the kettle on again
She has made me my last cup of tea here

All cups of tea with her from now on
Will be made by someone else
Or be bought when we venture out
But at least we can still do this

And we will

A Poem Where Richard Dimbleby
Makes An Unexpected Appearance
#973 / 12:10:2022

Finding the deeds for mum's bungalow
Literally opened old boxes
Old boxes I knew existed
But had never felt the need to look into

Always knew I could have looked
Any time I wanted to
But I had never wanted to. Simple as that
Mum and dad are mum and dad

My brother once found them by mistake
I knew I was born Christopher
He told me my surname was Goldsmith
Turns out it wasn't. Goldswain

Adoption papers, correspondence
Birth certificates, health reports
Treasury tagged together
In a creased manila Customs and Excise folder

And dad's handwriting
Capitals we could read easily
The rest – stenographed high lines and tiny vowels
That looked clinical but were anything but

I never thought of dad as a letter writer
But there were so, so many
Business like on the adoption process
Gently informative updates and always gratitude

"He is a happy little soul
Except when hunger calls
And brings great joy and happiness"

"Young Paul continues to thrive
He was one yesterday and is walking
But scorns talk of any kind"

"Paul is helping in the garden
Usually taking one particular tool you need next
Far out of the way"

"He looks like Richard Dimbleby
And is just about as garrulous"

Garrulous –
Excessively talkative
Especially on trivial matters

Some things don't change then

As If You Weren't Despised Enough ...
Wake Up And Smell The Coffey
#974 / 13:10:2022

Poor people are richer than you think
Proclaims a privileged politician
Proving ministers even nastier than you think
With each new damning statement of division

Separate From Birth
#975 / 13:10:2022

It's not like I didn't know
You can't Not Know
Biological fact
I knew I had a birth mother

Today I saw her name for the first time
And that changed things
Today I saw her words for the first time
And that changed everything

Valerie
Valerie Goldswain
You had never seemed real before
But you are now

Three handwritten notes
Blue fountain pen, neat and precise
Correct spelling and punctuation
But so much more

Seeing your letters brings home
That you actually sat at your table
With a pen and paper
While these heartfelt words flowed

They must have broken your heart
They certainly broke mine
Perhaps I cried as many tears reading them
As you did writing them

"I loved him dearly
And would love to keep him
And look after him forever
But circumstances are beyond my control"

"Please"
And the fact that the please is underlined
"Please make him
The happiest little boy in the world for me"

"Is he as hungry as ever?
Thank you for taking Christopher
Into your home
Bless you all"

"I can't tell you how grateful I am
P.S. Give Chris a kiss and a cuddle from me
Bless you all
Valerie"

Valerie Goldswain
Thank you
Without you I would never have had
The love of mum and dad

Two of the most special people ever
But Valerie
Forgive me for not really thinking about you
Until now

"Typing this through tears. Completely broke my heart this morning.
These poems may be the most beautiful poems you've ever written."
Neil Mitchell

When Is A Door Not A Door ...
#976 / 14:10:2022

A door I knew existed
To a room that I left long ago
Not so much resisted
More, I didn't need to know
For years and years no burning urge
To find out who we are
But the door that once was locked is now ajar

For everything, a season
For everything, a time that's right
Combine to give a reason
To open what was once shut tight
Never ventured thus before
Never trod this far
And the door that once was locked is now ajar

All secrets yet untold
Uncertainty may lie behind
Consequences to unfold
But ready now with open mind
I hold the keys within my hand
No need for no crowbar
And the door that once was locked is now ajar

A lifetime lies beyond
One almost gone, unrecognised
Not sure how I will respond
The tears already in my eyes
A universe that's new, a chance
To find a brand new star
And the door that once was locked is now ajar

How far this door will open
Will be revealed in time
How much my heart is broken
Depends on what there is to find
Memories, as yet unknown
How deep this reservoir
And the door that once was locked is now ajar

The Krazy Kwasi Karteng Kartoon Krackpot Kalculator
#977 / 15:10:2022

It's magical and mythical
Most marvellous creation
Mysterious and mystical
Guaranteed to save a nation
No-one knows just how it works
Not even its creator
The Krazy Kwasi Karteng Kartoon Krackpot Kalculator

Defies the views of experts
With built-in analytics
Internal logic systems
That don't deal in specifics
Completely independent
Requires no regulator
The Krazy Kwasi Karteng Kartoon Krackpot Kalculator

You simply could not make it up
Except the fact he did it
Can't comprehend the working out
Not least because he hid it
No mere work of fiction like
The Great Glass Elevator
The Krazy Kwasi Karteng Kartoon Krackpot Kalculator

Only has two buttons
No need for anymore
Addition for the rich
Subtraction for the poor
A tap-tap here, a tap-tap there
For the fiscal mass debater
The Krazy Kwasi Karteng Kartoon Krackpot Kalculator

No memory recall at all
No sign of the times
No button for division
Or for the equal sign
An extra button labelled
Rich Tax Renumerator
The Krazy Kwasi Karteng Kartoon Krackpot Kalculator

The madman of the maths
The crazy vacant grin
Glasses glazed and fazed
At the numbers massaged in
Self-satisfied and glassy-eyed
The smile of an alligator
The Krazy Kwasi Karteng Kartoon Krackpot Kalculator

It's got the bells and whistles
It pings and dings and makes a noise
Rotates, vibrates and calculates
For boys who like to play with toys
No real sign of growth at all
From this simulator
The Krazy Kwasi Karteng Kartoon Krackpot Kalculator

Tap five and eight, double oh, eight
Then turn it upside down
An adequate description
To the answers that he's found
Still he cannot handle
The budget hot potato
The Krazy Kwasi Karteng Kartoon Krackpot Kalculator

Uh-oh, oh no – out of control
Nothing's making sense
Disrupting and bankrupting
Changing pounds to pence
Someone has to take the blame
So goodbye! See you later ...

All thanks to – you know who
And his nothing backed up, crocked and cracked up
Self-imploding, overloading, complete collapsing and exploding
Kamikaze self-destructing, booby trapped and self-corrupting
Krazy Kami Kwasi Karteng – see his car now fast departing
Krazy Kami Kwasi Kancellor – yet another new ex-chancellor
Thought it was his calculator ...
Instead it's Truss's Terminator and Chancellor Regenerator

Sunday Is Not A Day For Cynicism
#978 / 16:10:2022

Somehow
It doesn't feel right
To be cynical on a Sunday

Maybe it's the childhood Methodist in me
When Sunday was a different day
Shops shut
No real playing out the same
A day of rest
Unless you went to church

But Sundays were different
And I can't shake that now
Don't want to either

So, this is a reflection
Of all that has gone before this week
And all that the coming week may offer

A time to stop
Think
Pray even

Last night
I shared a room full of laughter
Warm and from the heart
Soulful, thoughtful, nostalgic, real
And it is that
I reflect on now when writing this poem

About not being cynical on a Sunday

A Truss With No Support
#979 / 17:10:2022

Like underpants with no elastic
Nothing tight or taut
Loose and free for all to see
A truss with no support

Beyond repair, shot full of holes
Like a damaged jockey short
Ripped and torn out, a tattered, worn out
Truss with no support

Swinging one way then the other
No control of any sort
Allowed to dangle, every angle
A truss with no support

More than dirty washing aired
Swayed and frayed and fraught
Bruised and blue and all on view
A truss with no support

Too late to stop the bollocks now
Too late to be caught
Avert your eyes, you can't disguise
Problems of this shape and size
You can't fix, revitalise
Nothing now that fortifies
A truss with no support

Unaware Of Sharks
#980 / 18:10:2022

Out of her depth, still trying to swim
Sinking and drowning, still claiming she'll win
Oblivious to the sharks all around her
Poor Liz Truss – the human flounder

Government Policy Affects The Poet
#981 / 19:10:2022

Was once a sonnet
Now, not even a haiku

That Ever-Sinking Feeling
#982 / 20:10:2022

Confusion, carnage, chaos
Another resignation
Yet another low
In this failing situation

An embarrassment of glitches
A frightening conclusion
How bad must things be if
Grant Shapps is a solution?

Direction-less and mutinous
A ship in self-made heavy weather
Some rats have gone, some still to go
They're not in this together

"We've never had it so bad"
To misquote a well-known phrase
Just another day in parliament
In these deep depressing days

When A Teatime BBC Quiz Show TV
Reflects The State Of National Politics
#983 / 21:10:2022

A pyramid with no apex
A pen without a nib
A square without four corners
An arrow with no tip

A rounded winkle picker
A dunce's bowler hat
A traffic cone that's not a cone
A witch's hat that's flat

An ice cream cone that drips right down
A porcupine without its spines
A crocodile that has no teeth
A football team lost every time

A unicorn without a horn
A clawless tabby cat
An elephant without its tusks
A fangless vampire bat

A screw that will not screw
A nail that can't be hammered in
The bottom half of a Christmas tree
A shark without a dorsal fin

Concorde with no nose
A swordfish with no sword at all
A cutlass made of rubber
A hedgehog that is bald

A roasting fork without its prongs
To test the Sunday joint
I could go on and on and on
But just what is the …

Surely Not ...
#984 / 22:10:2022

All the fun of a live cartoon
A brand new comic returning soon
Jokes and japes and jests and joy
With Boris The Bounce Back Boomerang Boy

The circus soon comes back in town
You cannot keep a good clown down
Yoyo Bojo – do enjoy
Boris The Bounce Back Boomerang Boy

Fun and frolics, howls and wowsers
Laugh at those exploding trousers
Custard pies and cakes ahoy
Boris The Bounce Back Boomerang Boy

A joke not funny the first time round
Even less so with this clown
Surely even they won't re-employ
Boris The Bounce Back Boomerang Boy

Still far from the real McCoy
A bounder and his saveloy
No time for the hoi polloi
Claim your Halloween fright wig toy
Boris The Bounce Back Boomerang Boy

A Poem With The Word 'Hallelujah'
In It Because It's Sunday
#985 / 23:10:2022

Hallelujah! All rejoice
The one rejected's now the choice

The back-up, not the Rolls Royce
Not the hare – the tortoise

The one who didn't win the race
The one who didn't keep the pace

The one you didn't want in place
The substitute, just in case

Got the petard, here's the hoist
The one who lost is now the choice

Hallelujah?
All rejoice?

The Shame Of The Certified Names
#986 / 24:10:2022
After Michael Fabricant tweeted that Boris has the one hundred certified
supporters. Certified indeed.

The shame of the certified names
Who signed on the line for more of the same
Ignoring the past, the lies and the blame
The shame of the certified names

Claiming such honourable aims
When not so long back you were fanning the flames
Because of the failings, the parties and games
The shame of the certified names

The utter contempt and total disdain
Trying to cover up previous stains
You must think us all without any brains
The shame of the certified names

Trust – a commodity flushed down the drains
How can you honestly seek to explain
That a failure is now the solution again
The shame of the certified names

He may have withdrawn from the latest campaign
Timing and numbers and spurious claims
But the fact that he thought it was right still remains
That – and the shame of the certified names

**If Limericks Seem The Best Way
Of Summing Up The Current Political Situation
There Must Be Something Wrong**
#987 / 25:10:2022

The one that they didn't first want
Is now leading us from the front
That choice wasn't first
It could have been worse
It could have been Jeremy Hunt

Now I am no statistician
Likewise, no mathematician
But you cannot unite
If there's three in a fight
The only solution's division

Three and then two and then one
Boris and Penny, now gone
Rishi is left
But is he the best
If he lost but now he has won?

It can't be a brand new beginning
When the one first rejected is winning
You cannot disguise
He was part of the lies
Another untruth they are spinning

"I wish there was an applause button." *Sarah Addis*

This Latest PoeM
#988 / 26:10:2022

This latest poem
Is written with integrity and humility
And strives to rhyme those words
With stability and unity
But not in a way that's recognisable
Or natural
Or flows

This poem
Has already been rejected
But is now accepted
As the one true solution
Amidst all of this confusion

This poem
Has no irony whatsoever
But seeks to distance itself
From the narrative
It not only created and perpetuated
But the shortcomings
It was inherently part of

This poem
Is totally acceptable for Mother's Day
Why?
Because it has no
Man
Date
Whatsoever

This is the poem
You didn't really want
But got anyway

This poem
Doesn't care what you want
It just wants to be the first in the book
For now, anyway

Kestrels And Other Friends
#989 / 26:10:2022

The AA Book Of British Birds
Courtesy of the Reader's Digest
And my parents' bookshelf

The hours I spent copy-drawing birds
Usually in black and white
Mostly birds of prey and carrion

It was the hooked talons I liked
The sharp vicious beaks
And the dark shadowed eyes

Sat at the kitchen table
Pencil or black biro
And the blank sides of dad's work paper

Very rarely had a blank pad of our own
Usually scraps of wallpaper
Or office paper

Flicking through the pages now
I recognise the look of that Buzzard
The stance of the Kite and darkness of the Merlin

The others too that trip off the tongue
Kittiwakes and Corncrakes
Pigeons, Wigeons, Bitterns and Siskins

Names I recognise after all these years
But now it is my desk, not my parents' kitchen table
And I have all the paper I need

"Oh wow! I did the same." *Liz Million*

**Oh Rishi, Those Words Didn't Last Long Did They
When You Gave Suella Braverman Her Job Back ...**
#990 / 27:10:2022

Disappointment with this appointment
No utility of your humility
Just the brevity of your integrity

Echoes Of A Bunnyman
#991 / 28:10:2022

I am reading another book
About another man in another band
A band I've always been aware of
But were never a favourite

Not because of his guitar
More due to the singer's general gobbiness
I somewhat took against him
And ignored them

Yet now I am drawn in
By the voice of the guitarist
Reference points and recognition
Recollection and therefore connection

And, as such, I also find myself
Re-evaluating the voice of the singer too
Different ears, a different time
A different approach

Listening to songs more closely
Realising that I like them
Much more than I ever thought
And they are not just of that era

Music
The gift that keeps on giving
When you keep on listening
The magic happens

Glamla Motown
#992 / 29:10:2022

Sorting through my CD collection
Yes, I'm that old
I realise I have mislaid
At least two favourite compilations
Lent them out
To whom, I cannot recall

I have all the tracks elsewhere
But that's not the point
I miss the CDs and their cover pictures
eBay and three days later
We are together again
Old friends

Glam Greats 1 and 2
Forty songs from my youth
Of course, the mighty Slade are there
With Sweet, Mud and Suzi
Wizzard, The Rubettes, Showaddywaddy, T-Rex
Even The Glitter Band and Barry Blue

These are the people's songs
The ones we stomped along to
Now, conveniently forgotten or pushed aside
As glam is remembered through the eyes
Of the art school boys
Where Bowie, Ferry and Bolan are cast as kings
The rest, clown princes

But, to misquote Sparks
This town is big enough for the all of us

This town is
Glamla Motown

Whole Lot Of Shaking Going On And On And On
#993 / 29:10:2022

Jerry Lee Lewis
Goodness gracious

Those words sound ever so polite
Until they are followed by your rock and roll holler

And for that alone
Those flames will burn forever more

The Porcelain Tortoise, The Playing Cards,
Petanque And The Beatles Tape That Wasn't
#994 / 30:10:2022

The porcelain tortoise with removable shell
Now sits on my desk as I write this

It has lived in dozens of places over the decades
For as long as I can remember
Windowsills, mantlepieces, fireplaces, hearths, tables
It's just always been there, always

Remove the shell and there is a space
Probably safety pins for mum once
But now it is empty
Apart from dust and memories

Like the battered sets of cards
"Wot!", Lexicon, Sevens and "Pit"
Rules are hazy – or invented by dad
But what I recall the most
Are the hours around the tables or on the living-room floor

Shouting during the "Pit" market-place
(And was it the bull or the pig no-one wanted?)
Collecting stars or squares in "Wot!"

And the psychedelic master card
That looked like the background of the BBC Test Card
Trying to spell in Lexicon
And never beating dad at sevens
Family times, one more game, please
Winner takes all

And the unused Petanque
Bought as a present for dad
But he left us before he could cheat or beat us

Plus the Beatles cassette
That is not a Beatles cassette
The first tape I ever bought
The Beatles Golden Songs
Performed by Studio Five Orchestra singers and Choir
I should have known it wasn't rock and roll music

At seventy-nine pence from a downstairs rack
In Rumbelows or Owen Owen
I thought I was getting value for money
But I wasn't
At least I got to know the songs
And still do
The proper versions now

Items from the past
Present
And correct

Pleasant and collected

Dead Dog In A Suitcase
#995 / 31:10:2022
This comes from a story I heard about a woman who'd looked after her neighbour's dog. The dog collapsed and died in a park so she left the body in some bushes, went back to her neighbour's house and got a suitcase. She put the body in the case, but when she got to an underground station had trouble getting through the ticket barrier. A gentleman offered to help so she passed him the case ... and he stole it!

I'm an opportunist thief
Take my chances while I can
Do unto others – my belief
I'm just that kind of man
Crafty, cool, quick and brief
Spontaneous in my plan
Nicked some strange stuff in my time
But this takes weirdest pride of place
The day I lifted up a stiff ...
A dead dog in a suitcase

A dead dog in a suitcase
And my immediate thought is
Why's a canine in this space
With a case of rigor mortis
The legal question that I'd face
If I should get caught is
Who left this cur, this lifeless fur-bag
It is a disgrace
It can't be right, squeezed in so tight
A dead dog in a case

A dead dog in a suitcase
Is not where it belongs
A dead dog in a suitcase
This animal's rights are wronged
This fruit-case with a loot case
Of decaying dead dog pong
A marble gaze of lifeless eyes
From this once friendly face
Seem puzzled, asking why am I
A dead dog in a case

A dead dog in a suitcase
Certainly not dozing
The odour that it emanates
Shows that it's decomposing
And the buzzing that vibrates
Means that this lid needs closing
Of course you shouldn't see a corpse
Cramped in such a space
The hapless mutt that has been shut
A dead dog in case

A dead dog in a suitcase
And this hound I've found
Won't beg or sit or heel or race
Just plays dead lying down
No balls to fetch, no sticks to chase
It should be underground
No more barking in the park
There's nothing to replace
No more walkies after dark
A dead dog in a case

A dead dog in a suitcase
Deceased, defunct, departed
A dead dog in a suitcase
I'm in territ'ries uncharted
A dead dog in a suitcase
I don't know what I've started
Maybe there's a market for
Illegal post life trades
Of dead ex pets cos who expects
A dead dog in a case

Or a kitten in a clutchbag
A parrot in a purse
A budgie in a briefcase
Just what could be worse
A rabbit in a rucksack
A mynah bird in a man bag
A goldfish in a glasses case
A hamster in a handbag

A dead dog in a suitcase
You ain't seen nothin' vet
A dead dog in a suitcase
Wanna buy a dead ex pet?
A dead dog in a suitcase
Not something you'd forget
The off pat ex pet patter expected
What you see is what you get

Now I'm no taxidermist
But I'll tell you in earnest
It is just bad taste
Who gives a stuff, I've had enough
Of thievery and thuggery, doggy style skullduggery
Of this once cherished pooch now perished
Dead dog in case disposed
The dog is dead
This case is closed

"Just looking forward to the millionth. It may not make any sense
and the verses will be interspersed with shouts of *"nurse"* and
awkward bodily noises - but that in itself is poetry."
Andy Camp

Well, Hello Mrs Holder – Have You Seen My Marrow?
#996 / 01:11:2022

I haven't got a pumpkin for this Halloween
Instead I've got a vegetable that's big and long and green
It may just be the biggest one that you've ever seen
Ask me "Trick or treat" and I'll show you what I mean

> *Well hello Mrs Holder – have you seen my marrow?*
> *To carry it about I need a big wheelbarrow*
> *The talk of every town from Harrogate to Harrow*
> *Hello Mrs Holder – have you seen my marrow?*

Down at the allotment I'm the envy of my friends
All the men impressed how it bends and it ascends
Asking my advice and what I'd recommend
Cos they all know how it started but don't know where it ends

It wasn't just the fertiliser in the soil I'd till
Not just the manure from the horses that I'd fill
Into the ground and mix it round – but here's a bean I'll spill
The ingredient that's secret is the blue and magic pill

If you think it's like a cucumber you're in for a surprise
You ain't seen nothin' yet! – no courgette in disguise
No itsy bitsy teeny weeny yellow striped and green zucchini
The size of my first prize … bringing tears to your eyes

> *Well hello Mrs Holder – have you seen my marrow?*
> *To carry it about I need a big wheelbarrow*
> *The talk of every town from Harrogate to Harrow*
> *Hello Mrs Holder – have you seen my marrow?*

How it grew's a mystery that won't be solved by Poirot
The long and winding root that isn't straight or narrow
Oh yes I'm pleased to see you – please don't call me shallow
Hello Mrs Holder – won't you hold my marrow?

Just Get Out Of There
#997 / 02:11:2022

I never really watch it
And really I don't care
But you are no celebrity
Just get out of there

All the lockdown failures
And your sordid sad affair
Now you're prime time viewing
Just get out of there

If you have been elected
Then surely you're aware
Of serving your constituents
Just get out of there

Yet another bad decision
To go where egos dare
Such arrogance and gall
Just get out of there

When all is said and done
Seems fitting that you'll share
Your time with snakes and rats
Just get out of there

May the testicles of kangaroos
And other delicacies so rare
Leave a bad taste in your mouth
Just get out of there

It's really hard to swallow
At least you can compare
Just how we feel about you all
Just get out of there

A failed MP stars on TV
Just shows exactly where
We are as a society
Just get out of there

An embarrassment for all concerned
Everyone, everywhere
A waste of space and time
Just get out of there

The Legend Of Ronnie Radford
#998 / 03:11:2022
for Ronnie Radford

In days of old when football pitches
Were brown with mud and puddles
And looked like every local park
No bowling green emerald carpet
But a no-man's-land of equality
Everyday heroes were born
FA Cup fixtures where
Every underdog had its day
It wasn't just the Bests and Charltons

Giant-killing was commonplace
The magic of the competition
If it was your day then it was your day
Other names became legend
Names to shout when playing with mates
In your own Saturday afternoon matches
Scoring a long shot from distance
Was no longer just a Lorimer
But a Ronnie Radford special

From nobody to somebody
That one moment immortalised you
Forever in our football memories
Ronnie Radford we remember you
But in truth, we have never forgotten
And it wasn't even the winner
A thirty-five-yard worldie
Your moment of glory
Forever part of our story

Tired Of Banging The Same Old Drum
#999 / 04:11:2022

Different faces, different names
Same old problems, blame and games

Same old clichés loudly spoken
Same old promises now broken

Nothing new under the sun
Tired of banging the same old drum

Tired of shouting, tired of railing
Tired of pointing out their failing

Tired of chaos and confusion
Tired at the lack of no solution

Another resigns, another one gone
Tired of banging the same old drum

Tired of the comings and the goings
Tired of writing the same old poems

Tired of the soap opera we see
Like bad reality TV

Watching the farce they've all become
Tired of banging the same old drum

Tired of the joke that isn't funny
Tired of fat cats hoovering money

Tired of the food bank numbers rising
Tired of the fact it's not surprising

Tired of a party just for some
Tired of banging the same old drum

Tired of apologies and excuses
Tired of privileges and misuses

Tired of U-turns they keep on making
Tired of the liberties they keep on taking

Tired of how this country's run
Tired of banging the same old drum

Tired of the words we've heard before
Number Ten's revolving door

Tired of hearing the same old story
Tired that it's not mandate-tory

Tired of looking for the next bad pun
Tired of banging the same old drum

When all is said and all is done
Eventually a change will come

Nowhere left to hide and run
The future's only just begun

But until that battle's won
Guess what? I'll keep on keeping on

On and on and on and on
Banging the beat on the same old drum

"You did it bard. And every one worth reading. Lesser poets
would have given up. Thank you." *Jane Edgar*

Poem One Thousand
#1000 / 05:11:2022

We did it
Yes, *we*
Who would have thought
We would have come this far?
But we did it
Together

Don't want to go on about it too much
But consecutive poems, consecutive days
Written and shared
A thousand poems, nearly a thousand days

It wouldn't have happened without you all
You who liked
You who shared
You who encouraged
Day by day by day by day
You know who you are
I know who you are

So, thank you
Thank you thank you thank you
Everyone
These thousand poems are for you
Dedicated to you all

Be warned, however …
I hope you are in it for the long haul
I may not stop just yet
If ever

Until tomorrow, friends …

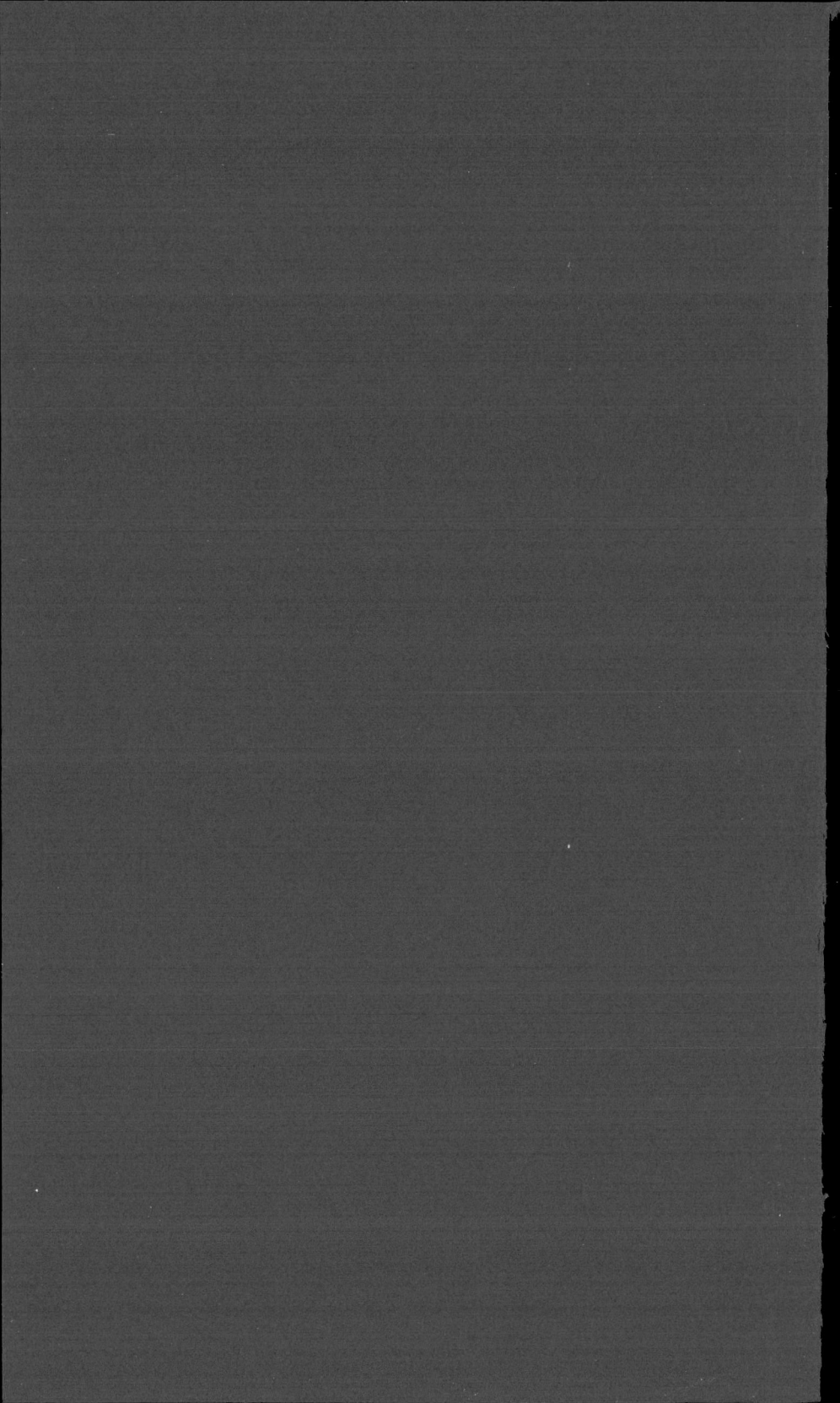